Headi1
HOM⌐

Heading HOME

MY SEARCH FOR PURPOSE IN A TEMPORARY WORLD

NAOMI REED

Authentic

British Library Cataloguing in Publication Data
A catalogue record for this book is available from the British Library.
ISBN 978-1-86024-853-5

Cover design by Paul Airy at DesignLeft (www.designleft.co.uk).
Back cover photo by Darren Reed. Internal photos by Darren Reed, Naomi
Reed, Bruce Wheatley, David Lowe and Warren Barnard.
Used by permission.
Printed and bound in Great Britain by Bell and Bain, Glasgow.

For Darren, Stephen, Chris and Jeremy
who have made each of our homes
a place I want to be.
And for all those (like me) who have dangled between
homes and asked the same questions, and
found the same answers.
My special thanks to Jennifer Gan whose editing gifts
are immeasurable.

All these people were still living by faith when they died. They did not receive the things promised; they only saw them and welcomed them from a distance. And they admitted that they were aliens and strangers on earth. People who say such things show that they are looking for a country of their own. If they had been thinking of the country they had left, they would have had opportunity to return. Instead, they were longing for a better country – a heavenly one. Therefore God is not ashamed to be called their God, for he has prepared a city for them.

(Hebrews 11:13–16)

CONTENTS

PROLOGUE

THE PLACES I CALL HOME

For a long time I thought that 'home' was a three-bedroom fibro house in suburban Sydney. The house itself was painted green, faced north and was positioned on the high side of the street. There were crimson roses in the front garden and gum trees in the back. From my bedroom window I could see the whole length of the street as well as the garden path and the swinging gate and the orange tree. The first thing I realised was that furniture arrangement was critical. If my bed was under the window, I could wake up and look at the clouds. If my bookshelves were under the window, I could read *Little Women* while the sun shone on my head. If my ballet barre was under the window, I could practise my pliés while watching the gum trees.

By the time I was 16, though, the desk was always under the window. That way, I could study biology (or think about studying biology) and keep an eye on the street – especially for the daily arrival of Darren in his 1970 Ford Fairmont. He kept arriving (fairly noisily) for six years and then we got married and moved to a two-bedroom flat near the hospital at Westmead. By then we had graduated as physiotherapists and were working at the hospital, so it was very handy. The flat itself was dark and small and had a view of the asphalt car park (which wasn't inspiring) but it was home because we were together. We cooked a lot of spaghetti carbonara and put

a painted Christmas tree on the wall and we wrote love notes
to each other and walked in the park in the evenings. But
before it truly became home we left and moved to India.

That was a shock. Our home in India was a 100-year-old
room near St Mary's Hospital, Khammam. We tried to put
photos on the wall but they fell off with the paint flakes. It had
a toilet in one corner, a gas burner in the other and twelve
holes in the roof. When the monsoon arrived, we discovered
that there was nowhere we could put the bed without being
rained on. We lived there for six months (and worked at the
hospital) and it wasn't completely home either, but we didn't
expect it to be; we were only there temporarily. We were on
our way to Nepal – a place where we planned to live for at
least three years. That would surely be home, because three
years was a very long time.

We travelled north to Nepal in September and it was
delightful. The monsoon was almost over, so the mountains
were in view and the skies were clear. We took a ten-hour bus
journey to Pokhara and moved into a small room on the
International Nepal Fellowship (INF) compound at the top
end of town. From our front window we could see red poin-
settias and thatched roofs and yellow butterflies. From our
back window we could see the Himalayas and a small section
of the teeming Seti River. From everywhere else we could
smell *dal bhat* and incense and buffalo. There were people to
meet and children to laugh with and a whole new language to
learn. The possibilities were endless.

But it was also hard. The water was cold, the electricity was
irregular and our grasp of the language was worse than irregular. We got many things wrong, daily. One day I asked the
shopkeeper for potatoes and he handed me yellow lentils.
Another day Darren (accidentally) tried to sell me to the man
walking up the mountain. The man stopped and looked at me
but he didn't appear to be interested. Even when we didn't get

things wrong, it didn't mean we got it right. We desperately wanted to talk to people but we couldn't. We understood so little – and that included thoughts as well as words.

One day, I went to the bazaar to buy bananas. I walked past the field where the women made cane baskets. I smiled at a lady with a heavy load of firewood. Then I stopped at the vegetable carts near the hospital. I pointed at what seemed like a nice bunch of bananas.

'*Pandhra rupiya*,' said the girl.

I knew my numbers and fifteen rupees was good for a dozen bananas so I handed over my coins without arguing. But as I packed them into my bag and walked away from her, I felt sad. What if I never really understood her? What if I never really knew what she laughed about or cried about or worried about? What if I was always going to feel foreign? What if I would never truly feel at home in this place, or anywhere?

That afternoon we gathered with the other expatriates in the thatch-roofed house on the INF compound and our English friend Steve began reading from Hebrews (in a lovely northern-English accent):

> All these people were still living by faith when they died. They did not receive the things promised; they only saw them and welcomed them from a distance. And they admitted that they were aliens and strangers on earth. People who say such things show that they are looking for a country of their own. If they had been thinking of the country they had left, they would have had opportunity to return. Instead, they were longing for a better country – a heavenly one. Therefore God is not ashamed to be called their God, for he has prepared a city for them. (Heb. 11:13–16)

'That's what we are,' he said, smiling. 'We're all aliens and strangers here in Nepal. We can't speak, we can't understand, we can't do the right things or say the right things. We're foreign and it feels awful. Some days, we just wish we could go home, or go back to the countries that we've left. And then other days, we don't even know where home is any more.'

I nodded and agreed with him. 'But what if God wants to teach us something new?' he said. 'What if we're here in Nepal to learn something new . . . that maybe wherever we are – in England or Australia or Germany or Hong Kong – we're all aliens and strangers? What if we're here to learn that 'home' is something different altogether? And what if, once we learn it, it changes the way we live, forever?'

I looked out of the window and agreed with him, in a theoretical kind of way. Outside the window, there was a Nepali lady cutting grass with her sickle. I could see the wrinkles on her face and hear the noise of her sickle. She seemed to know exactly what she was doing. She was at home. Then I looked back at my Bible and wondered. What did the ancients welcome from a distance? What were they referring to? Was it Yahweh's promise of the land of milk and honey? Or was it more than that? And what did it mean for them to long for their heavenly home, if they did? Did it really change the way they lived? And what did it mean for me?

Later, we went back to the bazaar and I bought another *kurta surwal* (the knee length national dress and trousers) and I smiled at the women in their saris and I bought oranges out of a *doko*. And over time, I gradually began to feel I belonged. A month later we moved out of the compound and stayed in a room with a Nepali family. The toilet was at the far end of the field. There were about a thousand friends and relations, all of them knocking at our door and wanting to talk to us. I got up early and watched Amma milk the buffalo and I learnt to make buttermilk and curd. It was good – all of it – the curd as well as the conversation.

Then three months later, we moved into our own rented house at the other end of town near the leprosy hospital. It was made of yellow stone and had four rooms and lots of windows. The toilet was outside but I could manage it in the dark. There were no holes in the roof (so that was nice) but we soon discovered that during the monsoon the rain poured in through the front door and flooded the house. We began work at the hospitals. We learnt how to do sign language and facial expressions as well as conjugate verbs. We made friends.

Then, during our third monsoon, our first son, Stephen, arrived. He was small and blond and gorgeous. I sat on our front porch in Pokhara feeding him and watching the clouds cover the mountains. It felt like home. We were there together, the three of us. Stephen learnt to crawl on the flat roof, laugh at the geckos and ride on the buffalo. Then he learnt to walk down the concrete path and rattle the front gate. People walked past the gate every day and they smiled and greeted us. They were friends from church, youth group and work. Usually they came inside and we drank *chiya* in the living room. We laughed and cried and prayed in Nepali and we still got lots of things wrong, but we belonged to the people to some degree because we loved them and they loved us. And it was good.

In the end, we stayed in Nepal for six years (punctuated by a few years back in Australia while we lived in three more homes and Chris and Jeremy were born), and it was all very good. During the second three years in Nepal, the five of us lived in Dhulikhel, halfway up a hill, on the way to Tibet. The three boys and I would walk up and down our hill during home-school and find strange bugs and shiny rocks and mud slides. We tried not to find leeches. All the bugs and rocks and tadpoles ended up in great piles on our back porch. The best thing about that home (our tenth) was the windows. They were all decorated in shiny red trim and they were perfectly positioned to take in the best view of the mountains – which meant that our youngest son, Jeremy, could name each peak before he knew the alphabet. And I didn't even need to rearrange the furniture to look at the view.

In those years Darren was busy teaching physiotherapy at the medical institute and riding his bike around the paddy fields. We all enjoyed our local Nepali church and made beautiful friends like Saru, Thakur, Jalpa and Srijana. On Sunday afternoons we would all pile on to the motorbike and head up our hill, yelling for more as we went over the bumps.

It was wonderful but it was also stressful. The trickiest thing about those years was the civil war. At the bottom of our hill there was a large army camp and we regularly heard bombs and gunfire. Every day, we looked at each other and developed a code for whether they were just practising or whether we needed to be under the bed. We had road blocks and shoot-on-sight curfews every evening. That meant that we stayed inside the house every evening and became very good at Scrabble, by candlelight.

The people were generous, the setting was beautiful, the relationships were deep, but the uncertainty was hard. During those three years we never really knew if we were coming or going – or if we were at home or not at home. Every day there was the possibility that the Maoists would attack or the political parties would call another strike or the king would take over the country and we would be evacuated. Every day we would look at our go-bag that stayed permanently by the front door. Were we ready to run? Did we want to?

More than anything, it reminded me that we were in Nepal temporarily. It was not our real home. Although we had wonderful friends and relationships, we might have to leave in a hurry. Even if we didn't have to evacuate immediately because of the war, we would still have to leave eventually. Our passports were all issued in another country, which meant that we had to go home sometime. So what did it mean for me to enjoy it richly, to plant down deeply in the community but at the same time be ready to go? What did it mean for me to cling on to people tightly but to our possessions and home very loosely? And could I actually learn those lessons well enough to be able to apply them to every other place we would live in the future? Could I, like our friend Steve, learn those lessons about home so thoroughly that it would change the way I lived, forever?

I'm not sure how well I learnt them or applied them . . . but I thought a lot about them. I thought about home and belonging, and what it meant for me to wake up in the morning (in the middle of the Hindu calls to worship) and belong to Christ and long for heaven, and to love the people in front of me. I thought about what it meant for me in a land where I wasn't known or understood, where the soil wasn't mine, the language didn't come easily and the cultural norms seemed impossible. I prayed about what it meant for me in the light of the view and the war and the go-bag and our friends at church.

O Lord, teach me what it means to be a citizen of heaven and of earth. Show me what it means to be both at once, on the same day and in the same country. And then help me to remember it, and to live it wherever I am.

Amen

I could pretend of course that the prayer worked perfectly. I could try to convince you that everything was simple and easy, every day – that somehow the Holy Spirit did such a glorious work in my heart that I lived the balance between heaven and earth (and Nepal and Australia) every day, easily. But it wasn't like that at all. There were difficult days. And the temptation during the difficult days was not to long for heaven (or to grow in my walk with Christ) but to simply long for our home in Australia: to imagine the green grass and the friendly people and the shining rainbows; to long for a place where I was understood.

So, whenever the water ran out, or the electricity cuts were worse than normal, or the monsoon seemed interminably long, or the motorbike stopped, or the Maoists forced another strike, or my home-school patience ran out, or there were weevils in the flour (there were always weevils in the flour), I would think about Australia. I would think about our real home with hot water and electricity and cheese and lettuce and chocolate and olives and friends . . . where I would belong and be understood and known and everything would be alright and I would never make an embarrassing mistake ever again.

In the middle of 2006 we did return to Australia and it wasn't like that at all. It wasn't immediately home. I didn't immediately feel as if I belonged or that I was understood or known. I spent years wondering why not, and getting confused by the answers. That's what this book is about.

1

NO CONTENTS INSURANCE

For most of April 2006 we were stuck in a hotel in Kathmandu in the middle of Nepal's revolution. Two million people protested outside on the streets and in response the Nepali king called a three-week daytime curfew. That didn't help of course. It merely meant that the people became more and more vocal and we were stranded, away from our home and belongings in Dhulikhel. The crowd below our hotel swelled and got angry. Tyres were burnt and broken glass was thrown everywhere. They kept it up for 22 days and demanded that the king give in and hand back power to the people. Then, in an unprecedented move, he did! Just hours after we raced the curfew to retrieve our go-bag (which we had hopelessly left in Dhulikhel), the king gave in and Nepal became a secular state. The moment the news broke, we were back in our hotel room and we stared at the *Himalayan Times*, speechless. Then we went up to the roof and stared at the crowd below us, still speechless. Two million people now gathered in the narrow streets, celebrating. That afternoon, we ate *mo-mos* with our Nepali friends and couldn't quite believe the news. We were delighted for them. It was the end of a ten-year civil war and the revolution had been primarily peaceful. It was incredible.

But even then, as I reached for more spicy *achar* and tried to follow the conversation, I knew it wasn't really my celebration. I was part of them, I was delighted for them, but I didn't fully belong. By then, we had been planning our departure for a full year, regardless of the civil war. Stephen was 11, he was ready for high school and we all needed to reconnect with our home and life in Australia. So, a week after the revolution, all five of us got on an aeroplane and flew away from the soaring peaks and paddy fields and the colourful bazaars. In an attempt not to cry, I reached for an in-flight magazine and a left-over copy of *The Guardian*. Neither of them were the slightest bit interesting, but I pretended to read them anyway.

Sixteen hours later, we landed in Sydney and gathered our bags and struggled through customs, and I wondered whether our Nepali spices were food or not. Then we walked out through the automatic doors – which opened by themselves. I nearly tripped over my bag as I looked behind me for the clever sensing device. Then all sorts of family members pushed forward to meet us, so we hugged them all (in order) and then bundled ourselves and our belongings into the back seats of their cars.

There were seat belts everywhere. The boys didn't know how to use them.

'Yes,' I said, leaning over them, 'it's what everybody does here. It's the rule.'

Then we were off, speeding along the motorway. I reached down and held on to the door handle quite tightly. We hadn't travelled at speeds of more than 40 km/h for years, so it felt like we were flying, as though any minute now we would be up in the air. Then I reached over and locked the car door, in case I fell out. All the other cars were going in neat straight lines, staying in their lanes. Nobody was using their horns, or avoiding buffalo and holy men; it was terribly quiet. I watched the cars for a while and listened to the silence. Then I glanced to my left and right and saw houses on either side of the motorway; they were big and clean and identical. But there weren't any people anywhere. I wondered how the occupants knew which house was theirs. Perhaps they didn't. An hour later, we stopped at Dennis's house in the lower Blue Mountains. Dennis is Darren's dad. He is lovely and generous and we had stayed with him before, so we knew which house was his. I got out and smelt the eucalyptus oil. The valley behind his house is filled with gum trees, and that night they were deeply sweet and comforting – just like my favourite Grandma or our last camping holiday. And the bed was very, very soft.

The next day, we went for a walk around the streets nearby, trying to remember where we used to live and wander and play. At first, I could hardly cross the road. I looked to the right and then to the left at least a dozen times, trying to figure out how fast the cars were going. Then, while we were still watching the cars, Chris wanted to know where all the soldiers were. Darren tried to explain to him that there wasn't a war in Sydney. I kept staring at the gutters; they seemed unbelievably clean, and empty. Where were all the stray dogs, and the cows eating cardboard? We passed a nearby oval where there was a large group of white children playing soccer. Jeremy stopped and looked at them. 'I've never seen that many white kids all in one place.'

'Me neither,' said Stephen. 'And do you know what's funny? Nobody's staring at us.'

Nobody was. We turned around to check, just in case, and agreed that it was very nice, but it was also strange. Weren't we interesting any more?

Then one of the boys suggested that we go to the supermarket. We'd been dreaming about it for years, so we were all keen. We found a small red basket at the entrance and began in the aisle furthest away. It was entirely filled with toilet paper, and when we saw it, we burst out laughing. We remembered the way our shopkeeper in Dhulikhel used to retrieve toilet paper for us, one roll at a time, from the very top shelf with a very long stick. We smiled at the thought. Then we turned into the chilled food section and couldn't cope with that at all. How could we choose between so many brands and flavours of yoghurt? And why would we *want* that many brands and flavours? In Nepal, if the buffalo were producing milk, then we were thankful. If they weren't, then there was no *dahi* (yoghurt). I decided that perhaps we should just buy peanuts, but we couldn't find any, so we left the shop.

Back at Dennis's house, he tried to teach me how to reply to a text message. I'd never used (or owned) a mobile phone in my life, so it seemed completely pointless.

'Can you just explain to me why I would *want* to send a text message?' I asked.

I'm not sure what he said in reply. Meanwhile, Darren was trying to remember how to open the automatic garage door and reverse the car out. That seemed complex enough in itself. We tried not to mention the motorbike or the hill that we had left in Nepal.

A week later we were still in shock and realised that we needed a holiday. Maybe that would help us familiarise ourselves with the Australian way of life and recover from the stresses of Nepal. We packed everything we owned into a borrowed car. Then we borrowed a tent and a mobile phone. I put my journals and books and precious things from Nepal into the car as well. If I tucked them into the back seat then maybe I could pretend we still had our go-bag nearby; or maybe I could read them while we were away and they would help me feel at home. The boys each packed a bag and we set off in a northerly direction.

The skies were blue and the people were friendly. We collected shells at Byron Bay and we watched the birds at Hervey Bay. We visited friends in Biloela and rode bikes in Yeppoon. We went snorkelling at the Whitsunday Islands and ran across the whitest sand in the world. Along the way we practised shopping and we went to the bank and we even began to read the Australian newspapers, trying not to be horrified by the way that scandal appeared to be news.

But mostly we observed, and that was better than nothing. The breadth of the landscape spoke gently to us and we started to relax. By day nineteen we felt that we could turn around and head south again.

The car took the inland route. By then, of course, the car was feeling like home – a moveable and safe cocoon from which we could stare out at the world. Not only did it neatly contain us but it also contained our most valuable possessions – our laptop, camera and my journals from Nepal. We were finally relaxing. On day 33 and 5,000 kilometres later, a (very useful) text message arrived to say that the tenants had moved out of our house and we could move in. We could move in to our own home. It was terribly exciting!

There was only one more evening to go. We drove into a camping ground in Dubbo and put the tent up for the last time. We planned to visit the zoo in the morning and then drive home. Finally! And this time it would definitely feel like home. The boys started drawing house plans and arguing about where everyone was going to put their beds.

'I don't care, so long as I get to sleep with Mum,' said Darren.

The pasta was good and the sleeping bags were cosy and we slept heavily.

At 6.30 a.m. I spent half an hour deciding whether I would go for a run along the river or not. The river was nice, but so was the sleeping bag – it's always the way when you're thinking about a run – but by 7 a.m. the run had won, so I got out of the tent and made my way across to the far side of the car, looking for my water bottle. But I got to the car door and noticed that there was glass on the ground. Bits of window pane were everywhere.

I looked up at the sky. Perhaps a branch had fallen on to the window of our cocoon and smashed it. There were no trees. Then I noticed that my handbag and money belt were gone from the car. I screamed. Darren crawled out of the tent and started running to call the police. I looked back through the remains of the window and saw that the camera was gone . . . and so was the video camera and the laptop. I started to cry. The car was still locked. Then I noticed that my black bag was gone, the one with all of my journals in it – all of my stories from Nepal, all of my thoughts, all of my memories, all of me.

The boys must have heard me because they also came crawling out of the tent. They pressed against me, not knowing what to do. But I couldn't speak to them; I just stared at the empty spots in the car, especially the place where the laptop had been. It held all of our photos, all of our memories of that other life, as well as all of my typed stories. Even my Nepali jewellery was gone – all of the earrings that I'd bargained for on crazy trips through Kathmandu bazaars – and my maroon sunglasses and Himalayan diary and little address book full of our Nepali friends. There was no more cocoon.

At that moment, a lady came over from the tent next door. 'What's wrong?' she asked.

Through my tears, I saw her short hair and her kind face. 'We've lost all of our belongings,' I told her. 'Someone must have broken into the car.'

She looked in through the car window and asked me whether we had contents insurance. It seemed a strange question to me. We had just raced a shoot-on-sight curfew in Nepal in order to retrieve our belongings from Dhulikhel. There had never been any such thing as contents insurance out there.

'Well,' I said, trying to explain, 'we don't really live here. We've just arrived back from years in Nepal where we lived through a civil war and a revolution. We don't even have a home, let alone contents insurance. That's why everything we had was in this car. Actually, all we have is this car and it's not even our car it's a borrowed car. All we had were the things inside this car.'

She started to look even more concerned. 'Were you with a Christian mission in Nepal?' she asked.

'Yes,' I replied, 'Interserve and INF.'

And then she put her arm around me and started to pray for me. She stood there by the tent and the shattered glass and prayed for Darren, for me, for the boys, for peace, for conviction, for the people who had taken our belongings. She prayed until I stopped shaking . . . which seemed like a very long time. And then she left. I don't even know her name. All we had were ten minutes, and that was enough; it was enough time for God to show me that he cared. He still loved me and he still sent people to hug me; even in my shakiest moments, he cared for me.

So I wiped my face with my hands and put my arms around the boys and we waited for the police to arrive.

Lord, sometimes it's very hard. The journey hurts and the tears stream down our faces. We lose the things that we loved – the people or the places or the belongings or the meaning that we attached to those things. And on those days it feels like we'll never stop crying . . . because the emptiness might never go away.

Please Lord, help us in our empty times. Remind us that it's OK to weep, or to feel angry or sad or lost or broken . . . because that's how we are.

And then remind us that you collect our tears in a bottle, that you care deeply about the things that make us weep . . . that you weep with us. Remind us that you're right here with us, that you haven't left us or turned your back or become busy or distracted with someone else or in another place. Thank you Lord that you are as present right now, as you've always been.

And Lord, we thank you that no matter how far away we go, or how many homes we've lost or belongings we've lost or people we've lost, you're still the same. You're still here with us, speaking to us, comforting us, encouraging us – through your word and your presence and your people. Thank you that wherever we are and whatever we cry over, you're always here and you always know the best way to love and comfort us.

Amen

2

THE MUDDY RIVER

The police arrived and started asking us questions. 'What brand is the camera? Does the computer have a serial number on it?'

I looked at Darren. Neither of us could remember. I could hardly speak anyway. I just knew it had all my stories on it.

'Are any of the items engraved?' Well, that was easier. No. We squirmed. We'd never even thought of it.

'And why were you carrying so much cash?' The policewoman looked at me as if I must be quite odd. I felt odd. I was a foreigner in Australia and I didn't know the rules. So I started telling her about the car being our home; that it was all we had. Then Darren told her that carrying cash was a Nepali custom – you either carry it with you or leave it under the bed as there were no banks in Nepal. And we didn't have a bed. We'd just run a revolution. She stared at us for a while and then she looked back at her notebook. She said that she was sorry but there was nothing she could do. She didn't mention the bed or the revolution.

'You could try searching the river,' she suggested after a while. 'That's often where things turn up. Not the cash obviously but maybe the journals.' Then she handed over to the fingerprint man and we headed off to the river. We headed off in a haphazard searching kind of a way, not in a running-happily-along-the-path kind of a way.

Two hours later, we'd done three trips along the river bank and were about to give up. The bag full of journals could have been dumped anywhere: in a bin, by the highway, near the shops . . . So why were we spending all this time looking in the river? We were miserable. We'd forgotten about the zoo and the home and the new life and everything ahead of us. All we could think about was the old life and the memories and everything behind us – or everything in the muddy river.

By 11 a.m. we were back under the bridge where the grassy banks merged into the mud. And that's when I saw it – an upturned Interserve medical form floating in the water. I recognised the red and blue charts. It had to be ours. It must have fallen out of my journal bag. I called to the boys and we all descended on the spot. There were a few other things floating: my Medicare card, Darren's empty money belt and a single page from my journal.

I reached into the water and pulled out the dripping page. The words had been blurred by the mud. I held it up closer and saw that I'd written a summary of Luke 10:1–24 where Jesus sends out the seventy-two workers ahead of him. He tells them to go because 'the harvest is plentiful, but the workers are few. Ask the Lord of the harvest, therefore, to send out workers into his harvest field' (Luke 10:2). And then I'd written a long description of how I'd felt on that April day in Nepal, two years earlier – I was so convicted to serve, and to persevere, no matter what happened. Then I'd quoted some great saint whose name I couldn't remember. 'The mark of any disciple is what it takes to stop him.'

Oh dear, I thought.

Darren began wading into the muddy water. 'If all of this is floating,' he said, 'there has to be more underneath.' He moved past syringes and old plastic bags, poking with a stick and trying to dredge up a book or a bag or any kind of missing treasure out of the mud. But nothing shone. Another hour later, his legs had gone blue and all we'd found was my lip balm, which wasn't very enticing. It was time to give up and go home.

We were all quiet on the journey home. The car headed in the right direction but our excitement had faded. The room plans were gone. We were hardly speaking. Every now and again one of us would remember something else that we'd lost: the list of email contacts, the new novel, Stephen's atlas, all of our deputation talks . . . It was hard to comprehend; it was a wave of nothing.

And then, four hours later, we drove into the driveway of our own house in the Blue Mountains – the one with the view and the picket fence and the glorious back deck. Years earlier, it had been our ninth home. We climbed out of the car. There was lavender in the front garden and daisies everywhere. Our feet made the same crunching noise on the front path that they'd made years before, in another lifetime. The key turned in the lock and we walked in.

It's not a very big house – five steps and you've seen it all – but that day we went exploring quietly. We noticed detail that we'd forgotten. Darren moved his hands across the fireplace. 'Wow!' he exclaimed. 'Look at the architraves.'

The boys found their bedrooms and then went out on to the deck to stare at the back garden. It seemed enormous, light and airy. 'We can play football,' they said.

I went to the kitchen and started opening cupboards and drawers. They were so smooth to open. Then I stared at the dishwasher. Imagine having electricity *and* a dishwasher. Then I moved over to the sink and let the water run over my hands. Imagine having running hot water.

In the corner of the kitchen there was a pantry. I opened the door and saw that it was full. Our friends from church had filled it up. I stared at the neat rows of food and tins and packets and herbs and spices, and there seemed more variety than had ever filled the little shop in Dhulikhel. Was that possible? Would we be able to eat it all? Or should we give it away to someone else? Surely there was someone who was hungrier than we were.

I left the kitchen and sorted out the mattresses and linen for the evening. We were exhausted. We were home, but we weren't really at home at all.

Lord, sometimes it feels like we're walking around in a vacuum. The external environment is familiar – the walls around us or our physical bodies – but inside our houses and bodies we're feeling lost and disorientated. We're missing the people or the roles or the belongings or the things that used to make us feel at home. And on those days we're sad. Our feet and hands keep moving, our eyes keep seeing the things in front of us, but we're grieving for the things we've lost. The weather and the flowers and the edible things in our pantry are all good but the ache still sits, deeper than that.

But Lord, thank you that you know us – you know how we're wired, you know why we're sad and you understand the moments when we feel like giving up. You, who cried alone in the garden, understand. You, who hung alone on the cross, understand. You, who watched your friends run away and your Father turn his face from you, understand. And you sit with us, telling us it's OK to feel sad and empty and lost, because when we love much and lose much, then it's right to feel sad. If we hadn't loved, we wouldn't feel sad. Thank you for understanding.

Amen

3

MY YELLOW CARDBOARD

The first three days back in our own house were very quiet. I started to hang up some pictures on the walls. There was no furniture, but that didn't matter anywhere near as much as the pictures. Then we bought a fridge and the first thing I did was put some old photos of our Nepali friends on the fridge door. It seemed more important than the food itself. I don't even remember plugging it in. By the third day Darren had found himself another laptop and he sat at the table staring at it. There was nothing on it. I began to unpack some boxes that we'd had in storage at Dennis's house but I couldn't remember where anything went. Did the glasses go on the third shelf or the second? Did it matter? And why had we ever needed that many mugs? Then I wondered about the weekend. Did we have anything scheduled? Without our calendar or email list or address book it was difficult to know. We didn't even have a mobile phone. Was anyone expecting us? I didn't know where to begin, or even why I should begin.

By the third afternoon, to avoid beginning, I picked up my brand new journal. A friend from church had given it to me the day before. It had pink roses on the front cover and was full of blank pages, so I began to write. I watched my pen move across the first page and then I looked up and stared at the gum trees in our back garden. They were numerous and green and they made a beautiful backdrop for the boys' tree house, but all I could see were paddy fields. I closed my eyes and saw women in red saris leaning over early plantings of rice. It was late June, after all. My mind travelled slowly back along our Dhulikhel street to the bazaar, past the tailor and the dough-nut man, the cobbler and the chicken lady, and as it did I kept moving my pen across the page and some of the stories came out again, as if seeing them in print would make them real again – or as if they hadn't really disappeared into the muddy river and I hadn't fallen into a vacuum.

As I wrote and watched the gum trees, I remembered a con-versation that I'd had with a friend six months earlier.

'Well, realistically,' she had said, '2006 will be a year of tran-sition for you. It will probably be hard, so maybe you won't do very much. Maybe you'll just live through it, feel it, breathe, that kind of thing.'

Mmm . . . feel it . . . breathe. That's a good idea, I thought to myself, remembering her smile and the way we used to run together along the Baglung road. But during the same conver-sation I'd explained to her that this was our fifth major country-to-country transition, so we were really good at it! And it should be the easiest of the five because every other time we'd moved countries we'd moved to an entirely new town. We had never lived there before, so we hadn't known the streets or the people or the customs or the things that people cried over. So, every other time we'd had to start from the beginning and work very hard to understand all of those things and make friends again.

But now finally, this time we were heading home to a place that we knew. We were coming back to a home that we loved and people we loved. We'd had cricket matches in the back gar-den and barbecues on the back deck. The soil was ours, the cus-toms were ours and the language was ours! It would surely be different this time; it would surely be easier.

But it wasn't, not really, not at the beginning. During the first week I spent a lot of time wandering around the house and wondering where I was. One day I went out to the back garden and looked under the house. There was an old basketball hoop lying in the dust that we had given one of the boys for their birthday. Attached to it was a large backboard with a caricature of a teenager on it. He had a big grin and sneaky eyes and I'd never liked his face. So I went back inside and got a thick black marker pen and then I went outside and defaced his face. I scribbled all over his stupid grin and his skinny neck and his bloated hands. Then I rubbed out his eyes until he would never see again.

Now, you have to understand that I don't normally do this kind of thing. I wasn't the kind of kid (or adult) that defaced the photos of political leaders or celebrities in the newspaper. But that day, I scribbled on his horrible face for about half an hour and then I went inside, feeling a whole lot better. But I vaguely wondered what I would tell the boys, which is one of the problems of being a parent – you're meant to behave. So I served dinner cautiously, worrying that I might be sent to the headmaster. Afterwards my lovely psychologist friend rang me. We talked about the kids for a while and then she happened to mention that sometimes after significant trauma – like living through a revolution, a major transition and a robbery – people can feel quite angry.

'Yeah?' I said.

Two weeks later, Stephen and Chris started real school. I'll always remember the day. After three years of doing (intense) home-school in the middle hills of Nepal, through monsoonal rain and Himalayan winters and piles of rocks and tadpoles, I was ready for them to go to school. I was readier than they were. It wasn't just the lack of museums and pools and science labs in the Himalayas, it was the daily struggle of coming up with enough ideas to teach them and then the extraordinary amount of patience required to carry them out. I still say that any parent who home-schools their children for extended periods of time deserves a whole lot more chocolate.

But that day, I dropped Jeremy at preschool and then walked the other two up the highway to real school and I felt strangely empty. After our goodbyes, I sat for a while, alone in the playground, and watched two crows fight over the remains of a child's lunchbox. The crusts disappeared. Then I looked at the classrooms and thought about our boys inside, without me, learning things that I knew nothing about. After three years of art lessons and geography and crazy science experiments, I'd moved off the stage, to a place behind the curtain. Nobody even knew where I was. Eventually, I stood up and walked back down the hill, alone, my feet leaving no mark on the pavement. I let myself into the house and the quietness spilled out into the hallway. I took off my shoes and tiptoed, in case I disturbed anyone. Even the walls echoed. I put my bag down in the kitchen, looked around me and wondered what on earth I was going to do next. I didn't know.

Maybe that was the hardest thing. The day after we unpacked, Darren found a copy of the local *Blue Mountains Gazette*. On page 52, there was an advertisement for physio work in a local practice. He rang and got the job the following day. Then the next week, he applied for and got a job teaching anatomy at Sydney University. It was the perfect combination of clinical work and a teaching role similar to the one he'd enjoyed so much in Nepal. Before we knew it, he was back on his bicycle, cycling down the mountain, and racing towards his new career path.

The speed at which Darren's life sorted itself out made the contrast with mine seem even greater. What was I going to do in Australia? And why? While I was still thinking about it, we had a phone call from another lovely friend at church. We chatted for a while and then she asked whether it was OK with us if she took our pictures and newsletters down from the church noticeboard.

'Well of course,' I said, without thinking. During our years in Nepal we had sent numerous photos and stories back to our church family which were then displayed on the noticeboard to encourage people to pray. But now they needed the space for updates on the hospital chaplaincy, she explained.

'Absolutely,' I agreed, watching the way the winter sun picked up the red and blue colours in our Nepali rug. 'That's fine.' Then she asked me how the boys were and we talked about other things. Ten minutes later I put the phone down and walked over to the rug. I felt the sun on my feet. But then I realised it wasn't fine at all. If we weren't cross-cultural missionaries serving in Nepal with INF any more, then who were we? Maybe I wasn't anybody at all?

The next week, a friend wrote to me and said, 'Naomi, it's a gift. Being in between homes and roles and ministries is a gift. If you see it that way and use it that way, you'll soon find out why.' I stared at his email and sighed. How could it possibly be a gift?

By then, other friends were asking me what I intended to do with my life. Would I go back to physio or would I take some more time to adjust to life in the West? Would I stay at home with the boys or would I do something else? And I had no idea. I wasn't sure at all. Some of them suggested that I keep writing or communicating somehow as they had really enjoyed the quarterly newsletters and the email updates. But I didn't know how I could do that. There weren't any more newsletters to write and my journals were at the bottom of a muddy river. I just didn't know.

A month later, another friend came to visit. She came all the way from Queensland to see me. So we sat on our back deck, drank a lot of tea and after a while she said, 'Well, the boys look like they're doing OK.'

We both listened for sounds of squabbling from the bed-rooms. There weren't any (momentarily), so I smiled and agreed with her. 'Yes.'

'But how is it for you?' she said. 'Being here? Does it feel like home to you?'

She's a very good friend . . . so I was honest. 'No,' I said, sighing. 'Not at all, actually. That's the problem. But I don't even understand why. Take the kitchen, for example,' I said, pointing.

She looked in through the windows.

'I remember it – all of it,' I continued. 'I remember where I used to keep the rice and the cereal and the way the dust collected in the corner of the pantry. I remember sitting at the kitchen bench and the way the telephone used to fall off the stand. I can even walk to the sink in the dead of night without bumping into anything. But I'm not at home.'

The best thing about this particular friend is the way she looks at you. You know that she understands without even saying anything. She has also moved house quite a bit, including interstate.

'Try drawing a picture,' she said.

The next day, after she went back to the airport, I drew my picture. I bought a large piece of yellow cardboard from the newsagent and began by drawing lots of circles. In all the circles I put people's faces – and their names, when they were unrecognisable. Then I drew places and things around them like the Himalayas and rivers and houses. You'll be pleased to know that I put Darren and the boys in the middle. And then it kept growing. By the time I'd finished, I'd drawn Australia, Nepal, India, England, Scotland, Fiji, Cambodia, Northern Ireland, New Zealand and Canada. That's where my friends are . . . and my body of Christ, and my stories.

At dinner time, the boys all came and had a look at my picture. They didn't recognise it immediately, so I had to explain it to them. Then I asked them how they were feeling about being back in Australia. Jeremy said that he didn't want to move countries again. He was worried that some of his treasures might not fit back on the aeroplane. But mostly he was working out whether the brown dribbly bits in his meat pie were food or not. Chris said that playing soccer every lunchtime was really fun. Then he checked again whether it was OK to drink the water from the tap after he cleaned his teeth. But he didn't want to talk about Nepal.

Stephen had spent more time thinking. 'It's not just one thing that I miss,' he said. 'It's everything. It's bus trips to Kathmandu, sleepovers with friends, INF conferences, monsoonal floods and . . .' he paused and fiddled with his fork, 'it's the way we always had something big to look forward to. Everything about our lives was special in Nepal and everything had a purpose – it joined together. We had friends who shared all of that and that made it more real. We don't have that here.'

'Oh,' I replied. 'Yes . . . maybe you're right.' I cleared the table and thought that maybe he *was* right. Our years in Nepal had been marked by purposefulness and we shared that with the wider mission community – the ones who were now living in my yellow picture. Even when the rain was ceaseless and the washing endless, there was still a high degree of purposefulness and identity. We'd invested so much simply to be there and every morning we woke up and remembered that – we could hardly forget it. Every morning there were the sounds of buffalo and roosters, bicycle bells and the Hindu calls to worship. But for some reason, waking up in Australia didn't carry the same urgency. It merely felt like I was here because I happened to be here. I was nowhere else, so I must be here.

The next month, we went on a re-entry retreat in Sydney with thirty-six other people who had recently returned to Australia. We sat in a circle and the facilitator began by asking us to describe our adopted country by using something on our body – either a piece of clothing or jewellery or an object nearby in our bag. Well that made me cry straight away because so many of our 'things' (especially my Nepali jewellery) had been stolen on the last night of our holiday. But over the course of the weekend I stopped crying and we all told our stories. Theirs were from Jordan, the Ukraine, Tanzania, Egypt, Papua New Guinea, Sri Lanka, Kenya, Thailand and Bolivia. We listened to their stories and enjoyed them, but the nicest thing was that they agreed with us.

One man, who had lived for ten years in Tanzania said, 'The problem is that I had dreamed of becoming a missionary doctor since I was a kid. That was all I ever wanted to be. Now it's finished . . . and for the first time in my life I don't have a dream.'

He was right. We'd lost our dream. That night, in a tiny room in Newtown, we realised that for our entire adult lives we'd always had a focus. Twenty years earlier, we'd been studying physiotherapy and planning our wedding. Then, a year later, we'd felt the urgency of overseas medical mission and applied to serve in Nepal. In 1993 we left for India and then moved to Nepal, which became our home and focus for the next thirteen years. There were years in between when we bought our house in Australia and finished our family, but Nepal was still the focus. There was always a bigger calling and reason to be alive. And now for the first time the focus was gone and so was the sense of home.

The next morning at the retreat, after our porridge, we all stood in a circle again and began to sing 'Great is Thy Faithfulness'. The sound of the piano reverberated around the hall and the voices filled the spaces. Then someone read from Psalms:

> O LORD, you have searched me and you know me. You know when I sit and when I rise; you perceive my thoughts from afar. You discern my going out and my lying down; you are familiar with all my ways. Before a word is on my tongue you know it completely, O LORD. You hem me in – behind and before; you

have laid your hand upon me. Such knowledge is too wonderful for me, too lofty for me to attain. Where can I go from your Spirit? Where can I flee from your presence? If I go up to the heavens, you are there; if I make my bed in the depths, you are there. If I rise on the wings of the dawn, if I settle on the far side of the sea, even there your hand will guide me, your right hand will hold me fast. (Ps. 139:1–10)

There was silence in the room that morning as we let the words wash over us. In the past we had always imagined that 'the far side of the sea' was in Kenya and Bolivia, Papua New Guinea and Nepal – the places where he had held us and been faithful through difficult years. And now, unexpectedly, in the silence, 'the far side of the sea' was where we were now – Australia – the place where he held us now, the place where he had us for a reason, the place where he was the focus.

Lord, there are times in our lives when we feel purposeless. The dream is over. We don't even know what to do any more, or why. We keep coming up with new ideas but they don't really compare with the dream we used to have, or the life we used to live. Then we start doing something but it's so hard to see the point of it or the reason you have us here. Maybe we've moved too far off the stage, or to the other side of the sea and it's not strategic or focused any more.

But Lord, when we feel like this – lost and directionless and lonely – please remind us that we find our living in you; we find our focus in you. Remind us that being in you is enough and that you are our focus no matter what country we live in . . . for you discern our going out and our lying down, you hem us in behind and before. You're the reason we get out of bed. You're the reason we make breakfast and stir the porridge . . . and every single day, as we settle here on the far side of the sea, your right hand will hold us fast. Lord, remind us of that today in new ways, we pray.

Amen

4

ULCERS AND UNDERSTANDING

There were moments when the boys surprised me with their insight. One day we were driving home from tennis and listening to the radio. The cricket season had just begun and there was a long interview prior to the game. The commentators were talking about the player Ricky Ponting and whether he would make a century or not.

'Isn't it weird,' I remarked, 'that this time last year we had no idea who Ponting was?'

Chris agreed. 'We didn't even know the cricket was on but now we do. And now we know who Gilchrist and Hussey are as well. We know all their names. But last year we didn't know anything.'

'Well, not really,' said Stephen. 'We did know something. Last year we were thinking about whether the Maoists were going to attack Dhulikhel or not. And then they did and we were evacuating, and then we got caught up in the revolution. That's what we were thinking about. It wasn't that we weren't thinking about anything.'

I looked back at the suburban scenery with the gum trees and the clean gutters and thought it was impossible to relate the two worlds: the cricket and the civil war; Ponting and the Maoists. But Stephen was still talking.

'The hardest thing is that we feel as though we understand them, the people here. We've learnt about Xboxes and computer games, cricket and Pokémon, and everything else they talk about. It's as if we can see through their eyes but they can't see through our eyes. They don't know what we're seeing – that's what's hard.'

He was right. They couldn't see through our eyes. Some days we could hardly even see through our own. There were moments when I longed for that community of friends who had known us in Nepal and who were now watching me from my yellow cardboard picture. So, a month later, when an opportunity came up for Stephen and I to visit friends we'd met in Nepal who were now living in Fiji, we jumped at the chance. Charlie and Linda were now working for an aid organisation in Fiji.

'Fiji!' you say. 'That land of palm trees and sandy beaches and hammocks swaying in the breeze.' Yes . . . that's right, that's what I thought. How delightful. And it was!

We started at the airport. I love airports. Stephen and I browsed in the book shop and then found a comfy seat in front of Gate 50. My shoulders relaxed and I breathed out. I can do this, I thought. This is so comfortable. And I vaguely wondered whether it was because I'd done it a hundred times before or whether the airport itself had become home? Does the airport become part of a long trajectory called home? From Dhulikhel to the Blue Mountains we'd spent time in the Everest region, the Tibet Guesthouse and the INF transit flat and at four airports. Do all of those places become home?

Then I looked up and saw an elderly Chinese woman saying goodbye to her beautifully dressed daughter. Their faces and gestures were so alike. Then the daughter covered her face in her hands and turned away, weeping. So did the mother. I couldn't look at them. It was too much of a reminder of all the times I'd stood at airports, weeping, saying goodbye to dear friends who had impacted our lives deeply, and then left. Airports are hard places, as well as comfortable places.

They're full of sadness and pain, as well as anticipation and reunions. And often it all comes together, competing loudly for our attention, until the feelings are too intense and we direct our attention to the snack bar and the schedule. How many minutes until boarding? How much are the chips? Do I have enough local currency? The mother took one last look at her daughter and disappeared beyond Gate 51. Stephen and I stood up to board our plane.

Fiji was wonderful. As I expected, the best part of it was connecting with Charlie and Linda again – friends who understood us and knew us, and had moved countries as often as we had. We talked and we laughed and we reminisced about monsoonal floods, journeys in *tuk-tuks*, the smell of the Bagmati river and the things we ate at Archanna's wedding. It was just as I had anticipated.

But the second-best thing was visiting the Suva women's prison with Linda. While Charlie was busy training local anaesthetists, Linda had been helping out at the women's prison. So when I got there, she was keen for me to visit the prison with her. And I was keen as well, in a theoretical sort of way. I really wanted to see what she'd been doing and the people she'd grown to love. But I'd never been to a prison before and the very thought of it was daunting, even in Fiji – or maybe especially in Fiji.

The day that we went was overcast and humid. The flame trees weren't shining as they normally did. We hopped off the bus and made our way up a muddy path to the top of a hill where we turned left and faced a huge metal structure. I began to think about the kind of women who needed to be kept in a cage like that . . . but Linda was talking to the guard through the grill and smiling and pulling out her pass, and then we were inside.

The gate clanged behind us. I could see rows and rows of concrete buildings – homes – with corrugated iron for walls and holes with metal grids and no glass at all for windows. Then, as we walked past them, I could see inside – more concrete, no carpet, no furnishings, nothing. Around us there were groups of women. Some of them were washing pots by the tap, while others were sitting on the floor sewing bits of grey material together. They were all dressed in a shapeless blue fabric that hung to their knees. Their hair was thick and matted, the way that afros grow when they're not cut. Their feet were bare and calloused.

While I was staring at them, Linda stopped to talk to a few of the women; she knew them by name. She was smiling and sharing news with them and they were chatting back to her, normally. But I just wanted to know how they ended up in a place like that? What had they done? Where had they been? Why were they here? And what were they seeing through their eyes?

Linda finished the conversations, and as we carried on down the pathway I thought I could hear singing. It seemed improbable in a place like that, but as we got closer I recognised what they were singing: 'More to be desired are they than gold, yea than much fine gold; sweeter also than honey and the honeycomb'(Ps. 19:10, NKJV). They were singing about God's ways and his heart and his law. We reached the room at the end of the building and we took off our shoes and went inside. There were already thirty women in the room, sitting cross-legged on the floor on bamboo mats, singing. We joined them. I could see the scars on their legs and the ulcers on the bottoms of their feet. Then I looked at their faces. There were holes where there once would have been earrings. Their necks and their fingers were bare. One of the girls next to me began to pick at an ulcer on her hand. Another one started crying. Linda began to pray and talk quietly. I noticed that they were looking at the Psalms so I opened my Bible as well (to try to stop staring at their ulcers) and then after a while Linda turned to me and said, 'Naomi, can you share something from your time in Nepal with us?'

Oh no, I thought, what have I got to say? What can I possibly say to these women? What do I know about their lives or what it's like to be locked up in this concrete, corrugated iron cage with no option to walk out through the gate again? How can I possibly understand them? I can't – I just can't. I haven't walked their walk.

But of course they were all looking at me, so I began to talk slowly about our time in Nepal and the way we'd come through the revolution. I described being evacuated from our home earlier that year because of Maoist attack and the seven nights we had hidden in a guesthouse on the other side of town. As I shared, I could feel it all again. The heightened sense of alertness and the way my body flinched at the sounds of bombs and gunfire. I remembered getting up on that first morning after we evacuated and reading Psalm 27:3–4 with the boys during home-school:

> Though an army besiege me, my heart will not fear; though war break out against me, even then will I be confident. One thing I ask of the LORD, this is what I seek: that I may dwell in the house of the LORD all the days of my life, to gaze upon the beauty of the LORD and to seek him in his temple.

And that morning in Dhulikhel, the truth of the psalmist had seemed so profound. Before that morning, the only place I had ever really wanted to dwell was in our cosy home with the red windowsills, and then, suddenly the home was gone and it was replaced by the house of the Lord. And the house of the Lord was deep and wide and good. So I told that to the women. I told them how hopeless I was and how attached I was to our cosy home . . . but for those short moments in my life, I had actually caught a glimpse of my true refuge and I had enjoyed it. And then I stared at them, knowing that they might never have even had a home, let alone lost it. But I kept reading Psalm 27 anyway, mainly for myself. I realised that the message was for me now, in Australia, as much as in Nepal. I needed to find the house of the Lord now – in the place where I was, surrounded by security and comfort – as much as I had needed it and found it when I was evacuated and homeless.

Then, very slowly, one of the older women spoke. Her hair was grey and her eyes seemed tired. Linda told me later that her name was Louisa and she'd been in prison for years. But she looked around to everybody else and said, 'You know, girls, we mustn't keep our eyes so much on our appeal date or on our release date, or the day we can walk out of here, we must keep our eyes on Jesus. He's our only hope. And when we keep our eyes on him, then we'll be really free.'

More of them started talking about God's promises and the hope they had in him, about dwelling in the house of the Lord forever and seeking him and waiting for him and singing to him no matter what happened. They talked about waiting for him to teach them his ways rather than waiting for release from prison. They didn't talk about needing to be understood or needing a home or needing a purpose or needing anything at all.

I sat there and looked up at the barred window and thought how easy it would be to focus on the release date, the chance to walk out of the gate and down the muddy path to the sea wall. It would be so easy to desire freedom, let alone understanding or purpose or home like I did. But they said, 'No, we may not be able to walk out of the gate, but we've got choice, we've got purpose. Even here we can choose to delight in God and find our security in Jesus. We can choose to wait for him, to meditate on his words day and night. Oh we've got plenty of choice. We can choose to be free.'

Lord, we've all walked a different path. We don't all sit in a prison staring at high security walls. We don't all sit in shapeless blue dresses waiting for an appeal date. But we all struggle with freedom and choice, purpose and being understood. So we find it astounding that you didn't spare your only son but gave him up for us that we might know forgiveness and freedom. We thank you for Louisa, for the girl with the ulcer and the one crying. Even now, they're sitting in Suva telling their friends that they're free to pray, free to hope, free to sing and free to go on in you. We thank you that you know their names, that you love them and you'll sustain them until you take them home.

And as we think about them in prison, we pray that we too would make decisions to find our security and purpose in you, today. Help us to keep our eyes on eternity rather than the government handout or the holiday in January or the day when we'll find something really important to do. On the days when we feel anxious and burdened by the uncertainty of our lives or the lack of understanding or freedom, help us to find our confidence and our refuge in you, help us to gaze upon your beauty and seek you in the temple, knowing that in you there's no uncertainty. You don't scratch your head and wonder what's going to happen next with the nations of the world or the finances of the world or the appeal date. You don't feel surprise as we do when we read the headlines or take the phone call. You don't ever panic. You already know the news, all that's been and all that will be, and you remain sovereign, in charge over the heavens and the earth. And we thank you.

Amen

5

HAVE YOU WRITTEN A BOOK?

After Stephen and I returned to Australia from Fiji things seemed easier. For starters, the dahlias were flowering in the front garden, which is always delightful. But as well as that, I thought I knew what the answer was. Instead of my focus being on what *I* was going to do in Australia, it shifted to considering what *God* was going to do in me and through me and despite me. It didn't matter where I was. It didn't even matter what I did. It was all about him and how he was going to conform me and teach me, through everything and anything that happened, even the boring bits – because that was so much more important than a definition of home or purpose. For as Isaiah 64:8 says, God is our Father, we are the clay, he is the potter; we are all the work of his hands.

As we walked to school that week, I reflected on the verse and a more appropriate answer to the question, 'What will I do in Australia?' I'll be the clay, and I'll remember who the potter is.

It was a good answer. But there were still hours in the day, especially on the days when Jeremy was at preschool, when I wondered what I should *do*. By then I'd begun to accept various voluntary roles with Interserve and INF, as well as speaking opportunities at churches and mission events. I loved being able to support the work in Nepal but I still longed to feel more 'at home' and less 'in between', whatever that meant. I think I wanted to belong. While I was still thinking about it, we went back to the library. It was almost summer, so I wore a skirt. Jeremy looked at me. He had never seen me in a skirt before.

'There's only one hole,' he remarked. 'Does that mean you'll have to hop?'

I showed him. We laughed. And then we walked together down the street to the library, hopping occasionally. The library was crammed full of wonderful books, so we stayed there for about two hours and then carried thirty of them home.

They were all good. They were full of worlds and homes and places that we wanted to inhabit. So we did, for hours. That's what Roald Dahl does to you. But as well as reading them (to myself and out loud to Jeremy), I studied each one of them for details about publishing. Sometimes, the most interesting page was the second one: who published each book and what year was it published and how many reprints it had had.

It probably doesn't sound all that fascinating to you (and I'd never noticed any of those details before either), but suddenly it became critical. I tried to show some of the publishing pages to Jeremy but he wasn't interested. All he wanted to know was whether Franklin was going to get a pet or not.

The background to my new interest is that I had begun to write while we were in Nepal. Afterwards, everyone asked me whether that was something I intended to do. Did I always intend to become a writer? 'No,' I would reply. Until our seventh monsoon in Nepal, I'd never written anything, apart from newsletters. After school, I studied physiotherapy, which was a science-based course, and I enjoyed helping people. I became very good at writing fairly illegible patient notes about the BKA in bed 42 who needed a PUF and SLRs . . . but no, I'd never thought about writing a book.

That was until our seventh monsoon – which was challenging . . . in every way. We had 120 days of rain, a civil war, home-school, a shoot-on-sight curfew and my closest Nepali friend was dying of a brain tumour. It was very difficult. I remember, at the beginning of that June in Dhulikhel, looking out at the grey clouds that were consuming the mountains and wondering how I would possibly make it through.

At the time, Darren was working hard, doing a rather wonderful job teaching physiotherapy to our Nepali students on the only national training course in the country. It was a fantastic opportunity for him to do sustainable work in a country with such limited health services, and I loved enabling him to do that. But the war and the rain and the home-school during those years meant that I was very home-based. The mornings were home-school, the afternoons were rain and the evenings were a shoot-on-sight curfew. And that didn't leave very much time in between. So I did the only thing I could do. I began to write.

As the days wore on, the writing became more and more important, almost necessary. Perhaps if I didn't write, I thought, the rain would consume me as well. I'd become part of the water cycle and I'd float out to sea (if that was possible in a land-locked country). So I'd have my ideas during the day while I was home-schooling and then at night I'd type away on the laptop, usually every second evening from 9 p.m. till midnight, as the rain thundered down outside and the power went off inside. I'm not sure whether you've tried typing by candlelight but it's not easy! You have to keep your head very close to the keyboard to see anything and then you end up with a really sore neck and have to go and find yourself a really good physio.

But I loved it. I really enjoyed the chance to think and pray and reflect. I thought a lot about God's purposes through seasons of life, especially monsoons. I thought about how he uses different seasons to bring about his purposes in our lives, and about what his purpose is through seasons, especially the difficult ones, where we can't see anything good coming out of them at the time. It is so easy to kid ourselves into thinking that God primarily wants to make things smooth and easy for us; he wants us to experience springtime all of the time. We even pray prayers all about comfort and ease, and could he please stop the rain or the war or the earthquake. Actually, if he had stopped the rain when I asked him to there would have been a massive famine across the entire Asian sub-continent.

So during that monsoon, I tried to stop praying smooth prayers and I kept writing instead. I found it incredibly helpful. There was something about trying to put my life in writing that removed it from me a little bit. It took it out from inside my head and into a more tangible set of words. And then, as I looked at the words, there was so much more to see of God . . . and there was so much more space in my head.

And the words kept coming! By August there were about 60,000 of them on the laptop, so I thought I'd better show someone. I bought a great wad of paper from the local bazaar and I printed out what I had and I gave one copy to Darren and another copy to the smiley friend with whom I'd had the transition conversation. I explained to both of them that I'd never written anything before, so please be gentle with me (because my skin was very thin), but any feedback would be welcome (I thought).

Darren read it first and he said he enjoyed it (probably because it was all about his life). Then he handed it back to me just before dinner and said, 'But I don't think that anyone else would want to read it.' And then my friend read it and she said, 'Naomi, I think it's a book.'

In September, some fellow Aussies in Kathmandu sent me a supply of *Australian Christian Woman* magazines that they'd been sent from Sydney. I fingered the glossy pages, thinking mostly about how shiny they were. That's what happens when you live through 120 days of rain and everything else that you own (or touch) is soggy. But I got to page 9 and I glanced down and saw a very small advertisement at the bottom, 'Have you written a book? Ark House Press is looking for manuscripts.'

It was quite a surprise. I wasn't even sure that I *had* written a book. Even if I had, I'd never heard of publishers looking for someone like me. I was sitting in the Himalayas in the middle of rain and war and home-school. I couldn't look for publishers online because our long-distance Internet costs from Dhulikhel were more than our monthly salary. So I just sat there and stared at the advertisement. Maybe I had written a book. How would I know if I had? So I sent the manuscript back with some visitors from Australia (with a long letter about how I was stuck in the Himalayas in the middle of war and rain and home-school) and then I carried on with our life in Dhulikhel.

So that's the background. But a year later, we were in Australia having just been to the library and I still hadn't heard anything definite from the publisher. I knew they had received the manuscript because they had sent me a receipt letter but they had also said that decisions regarding publishing could take up to a year. So that left me waiting and wondering. Perhaps it was dreadful? Perhaps I was kidding myself? Perhaps it wasn't a book at all? All of the above could easily have been possible, which is why I was studying page two of every other book I could find, just in case some further insight jumped out at me. Then I started making deals with Darren.

'Well,' I told him, 'if I don't get published by the end of the year, I'll go back to physio. I'll try and find a job.'

It must have been early September when I said that, so I was feeling confident. So was he. Anything could happen in four months!

But anything didn't happen for three months. I walked to the boys' school and I walked home again. I cut up cucumbers and watermelons. We went to the post office and the newsagent and the library and the pool, and it was all good . . . except that I was quite keen to have some clear direction for the rest of my life.

Then, at the end of November, the phone rang. I said hello. The woman said hello. She said that she was Jodi from Ark House

Press and she was calling to let me know they planned to publish my manuscript in May the following year. I put the phone down and screamed. I ran outside and called to our dog Millie. She galloped up the stairs and barrelled into me. It was the middle of the day on a Thursday, so there was no one else around to hug.

At first Millie and I just sat there on the deck and stared at each other. I cried a bit and told her that we needed to celebrate. So then she started to chew on the chair leg and I went inside and found some chocolate. Then I picked up the phone and rang Darren and my mum and anyone else I could think of who would listen to me. I was going to have a book on a shelf! A real book on a real shelf! As I talked, I looked out of the kitchen window and wondered why there wasn't a great big sign in the sky. Surely this was news! Surely everybody should know by tomorrow! But mostly, I just sat there and gave thanks to God, who is so much bigger than the sky, let alone a sign in the sky, or a bookshelf . . . and whose purposes are bigger than the stars themselves.

Lord, there are some days that are memorable. We get phone calls and they change everything. They're so unexpected. And we remember the dates forever because the things that come after them are so different to the things before. On those days it's easy to see your glory and your purposes; it's easy to praise you and it's easy to sing; it's easy to hug the people (or the pets) around us; and it's easy to look back and understand what you've been doing through 120 days of rain.

But Lord, help us to worship you on the other days, in the middle of the rain and the watermelon and the war, when we can't see anything or do anything, when we haven't got the phone call or the magazine or the news, and when all we hear is the noise of the gunfire or our own imaginations. Lord, help us to see you and praise you on those days – to be content in you when the answers aren't clear and the doors aren't open – because you're still the Lord even then and we trust you.

Amen

6

MAKE THE STONES STONY

November turned into December. As well as anticipating the New Year and all the new things it would bring, we also realised that we'd been back in Australia for six months. So I decided to mark the occasion by cooking a festive chicken *dal bhat*, with extra *dahi*. Then I got out a very large piece of paper (white this time) and spread it out on the dining table. I divided it into four sections with headings at the top:

1. The things I miss about Nepal
2. The things I don't miss about Nepal
3. The things I'm enjoying in Australia
4. The things I'm not enjoying in Australia

At this point, the boys looked at me suspiciously and sighed, clearly wishing they belonged to another family. But I smiled cheerily at them. 'Come on, it will be fun,' I said, handing out different-coloured pens. 'And it might help us to see that every place has its ups and downs. It's not just Australia or Nepal. Wherever we are, there are hard things and there are good things. It's the way it is and it's the same for all of us.'

So they consented briefly (probably because they knew there were still ice creams in the freezer) and started fiddling with their coloured pens. Darren started saying funny things about monkeys in the window until they all joined in. But we were remarkably consistent. We all enjoyed having Millie (even when she escaped and ran down the road at six in the morning). We all missed our friends in Nepal as well as the mountains, the motorbike and the monkey. We even missed home-school. None of us missed the leeches, the bombs or the gunfire. We were all fairly non-committal about school in Australia as well as work and transport. It just wasn't as much fun. But we really liked our friends and our family, our back garden and our ice creams. I liked my publisher. And that was about it . . . but seeing it on the page was certainly helpful, for me at least. 'So this is where you are,' the page said. 'Enjoy it.'

Along with December came Christmas. That was a surprise. We had spent six Christmases in Nepal and they were all uniquely Nepali. On Christmas Eve we would walk down the main street of our local bazaar in Dhulikhel and vaguely notice that there weren't any decorations or Christmas trees or nativity scenes or carols or lights or anything else, which is exactly what you'd expect in a Hindu kingdom. But then on Christmas Day in Nepal, the Nepali Christians would get together and celebrate and we would join them for a special *dal bhat* and spend the day remembering the goodness of God in sending his son Jesus.

So December in Australia was surprising. Every day there seemed to be more and more people at the post office, the newsagent and the supermarket near our house. There was a buzz everywhere, even in the car park. But it didn't look as though they were milling around enjoying the toilet paper aisle or even the choice of *dahi*. They all seemed terribly focused, as if they needed to get something perfectly right. The problem was that I didn't know what they were trying to get right. So I watched them more closely and tried to eavesdrop on their conversations (apparently you're allowed to do that when you're a writer). One day I overheard the focus in the chilled food section – two middle-aged ladies talking to each other about fancy cheeses, deli hams, chocolate nuts and condiments, and whether Auntie Beryl was coming for lunch or not. They were in Australia, doing Christmas.

The most confronting moment for me came one day when I had to go back to the supermarket because we'd run out of rice. That always involved walking past the budget shop on the corner. I should never have gone in, I realise that now, but I happened to notice that there were some very nice candles on the front shelves and nice candles are a bit of a magnet for me, particularly if they're purple.

So I walked in. In front of me there were enormous flashing Christmas lights, surrounded by gaudy green tinsel. There were blow-up snowmen that filled the entire back wall of the shop. There were huge red boxes, red Santas, red reindeer and red balls. There was plastic everywhere. There was even a Rudolph that moved and spoke. I might have coped with all that but the thing that tipped me over the edge was a tiny nativity scene right in the middle of all the plastic. It was very small – it was just Mary, Joseph and baby Jesus, one lamb and one shepherd. I probably should have been glad that it was there at all. Jesus is the reason we celebrate, after all. It was a good thing. But we had just flown in from the Third World and something inside me cracked. Part of me wanted to cry and swipe the things off the shelf, saying, 'Don't you associate my Saviour with any of that!' I didn't of course. I'm quite well behaved, apart from the basketball hoop incident. So I put my hand in my pocket and tried to back out of the shop, avoiding the reindeer and forgetting the candles. Once out of the shop, I slowly made my way back home across the car park.

Later that night, I turned on the computer, began to type and didn't stop until the fire inside me had found somewhere safe to burn.

In Australia, we seem to flood ourselves with profit-driven Christmas paraphernalia for as many months as possible.

There's nothing wrong with tradition and celebration and thankfulness, but there's something wrong when it's driven by indulgent and excessive materialism. Every now and again, the nativity pops up in the middle of it and we don't quite know what to do with it. When it does pop up, it feels fragmented – as if the nativity story is battling away on its own, vainly trying to say something meaningful in the middle of the red and green tinsel. But the nativity scene only ever existed because of the *bigger* story: the context of the whole work of God, who made us in the beginning of time and wants to be in relationship with us, who was unbelievably patient with the Israelites for thousands of years until it was time to come himself, in the form of his only son, so that our sins could be forgiven, so that we could be right with him, so that our emptiness could be met by relationship and intimacy, and so we, who were broken, could be made holy and prepared for heaven. And there's a very good reason why that's such a long sentence! It's a long story. It was never meant to be fragmented and it was never meant to be associated with excess.

So that night, in my angst, I wrote a story from the perspective of Mary the mother of Jesus. But I didn't imagine her as the young Mary by the manger, with the lambs. I imagined her as an older Mary, nearing 80, who wouldn't just remember the birth of her son and the feel of the swaddling-clothes. Surely, at 80, she would speak about his death and resurrection. She might even try to make some sense of it and speak about the sacrifice, the growth of the early church, the angel's promise or the difference it had made to their lives . . . or maybe she would just say how much she loved him. Maybe, at 80, if people had asked her to retell only the birth story, she would have felt sad. I would have, if it were me.

Stephen was born in Nepal and today, as I write this, he's 16. His birth story is rather dramatic and gripping, in a Nepali kind of way, and I retell it occasionally on request. But if people only ever wanted to know about his birth, and not his life or thoughts or experiences, I would feel sad. His birth was merely the beginning of his life, not the summary of it or the reason he lived. How much more upset would Mary feel if people only ever wanted to know about the manger and the shepherds and the sheep . . . and not the reason Jesus lived or the cost of his dying or the miracle of his resurrection. And how would Yahweh feel?

On Christmas Eve, after weeks of thinking and writing, I performed the piece at our local church service. I put a blue scarf over my head and disappeared into another century, and another country, imagining the story and the message – the story that began with the angel and finished with an empty tomb. It was as if I were there, wrapping the Son of God in a piece of cloth and laying him in a manger, and then some years later, watching his body taken down from the cross and then later wrapped by someone else and laid inside the tomb, lifeless. No wonder the sword pierced her soul. No wonder she cried. By the time word came of the resurrection, I could hardly speak, I was so moved by the truth and the wonder of it all: he was her son and he was her saviour and he was alive. And he was *my* saviour.

We sang again. Lots of people cried. I cried, too. But then afterwards they apologised.

'Sorry,' they said.

I looked at them.

'The thing is,' I explained, 'we cry when we stub our toes or when the cake flops or when someone says something nasty to us. Perhaps it's good and right that we cry over the love of God – who allowed his son to die on our behalf.'

Days later, I was still crying. Even an article in the *Sydney Morning Herald* set me off. I was sitting on our green sofa, in the living area, finishing off the last of the Christmas pistachio nuts, when I read a small reference to the crucifixion of Jesus.

I cried and cried and couldn't stop. I got up and walked to the kitchen to find the tissues, still crying. Then I went back and sat down and wondered whether it was because I was still in character, feeling it as Mary would have felt it. But then again, maybe I was feeling it because I was me. Maybe it was because the familiar story had become unfamiliar again and I was actually weeping for myself, as I needed to. My God had taken the punishment for me and he'd done it because he loved me, so I needed to cry and I needed to feel the truth of the gospel again, in Australia.

Two days later, I was checking the emails and noticed again the email from my friend. 'Being in between homes is a gift,' he said. 'If you see it that way and use it that way, you'll soon find out why.' I leaned back in the chair and thought about what he'd said. Then I looked out beyond our back deck to the bushy back garden and the tree house. It still seemed unfamiliar and strange, even though the leaves on the trees were now exactly the same shade of green as the paddy fields in Dhulikhel. But I wondered whether part of the gift was being able to see the familiar in fresh and unfamiliar ways. What if the gift was being able to see life and the gospel and people in new and fresh ways, and then to be able to put that into words for others? Perhaps he was right. As soon as the thought came, I knew that I wanted it, desperately. I wanted to make the stones stony again. I wanted to make the truth gripping again. I wanted it! And later that night as I explained it all to Darren I realised that it was the first time since arriving back in Australia that I was feeling excited about getting out of bed in the morning.

Lord God, we sit here today and know that we've heard the Christmas message before . . . we've heard it a hundred times. We've sat in churches and read the gospel accounts and sung all the carols and, in fact, we know it so well that there have been times when we've stopped listening. We've felt a little bit bored . . . and in that moment we've gone back to planning our Christmas dinner and condiments. Please forgive us . . . forgive us our tendency to distraction, for our tendency to reduce your message into fragments and for our tendency to imagine that we can package it in between the tinsel and the baubles. Lord, forgive us . . . for being bored by a message that was never meant to be boring – a message that was life and forgiveness and hope and restoration forever. Please make the familiar unfamiliar again. Please help us to see your plan and your purpose in fresh ways. Help us to imagine the feel of the swaddling-clothes and the sound of the soldiers and the smell of the empty tomb and to know deeply that it was for us, it was the only way you could save us. Help us to cry over the cross, without apology. Help us to say thank you again. Help us to be stunned that the veil was removed, the curtain torn and that our secret and shameful thoughts can no longer keep us from you. Help us to know deeply that it wasn't because we were worthy (or because we found all the right cheeses or candles or wrapping paper) but because you loved us. And we pray today that our praises would spring from that place of fresh wonder and delight.

Amen

7

THE OUTSIDER

The week after Christmas we drove three hours south of Sydney to visit Mum and Keith in their country town of Braidwood. It was the first time we'd travelled those roads for four years, so we were surprised by how dry the landscape appeared. On either side of the highway there were fields of brown dirt, broken only by occasional tufts of dry grass. They hadn't had rain for years. All the sheep seemed to have disappeared and gone elsewhere in search of food. But the fields just sat there waiting interminably for clouds to appear on the horizon and bring change. They didn't know how long they would have to wait.

Somehow, as we drove past Goulburn and then Lake Bathurst and Tarago, I related to the fields. I'd had rain before, in Nepal, I'd struggled through monsoons and sadness and uncertainty, but I'd had rain and the rain had been good. Maybe it was the actual difficulties of war that had helped me in my understanding of God, in my faith and in my awareness of his presence and purposes. I'd clung on to him because I'd *had* to . . . but now I was in a dry land again, where the challenges seemed more subtle but perhaps greater. Maybe I didn't need to cling on? Or maybe I needed to cling on out of conscious decision rather than out of dire necessity. And that was much harder. Maybe that's why I felt so in between.

But I had also felt the first drops of rain – and there were more to come.

After our time in Braidwood, we spent a few days at the beach and in Canberra. The first thing I noticed was how relaxed everyone appeared. At Batemans Bay a man in a kayak pushed dreamily past us on the water. Then a family nearby began making sandcastles. At Lake Burley Griffin children biked past us. There were joggers and lovers and babies in prams. Some of them moved quickly and others meandered. After a while, we joined them and became part of the culture of leisure. We swam and biked and rejoiced with them. Apparently, that's what people do in January in Australia. It's summer, and Christmas is over and everything has been achieved – presents, food, tasks and greetings – with varying levels of success. But in January it's all about relaxation. Relaxation is easy and it's even warranted. Maybe it becomes the higher aim.

The boys made sandcastles. Millie made holes. But as we relaxed, I wondered quietly what Srijana would think. In Dhulikhel leisure wasn't ever warranted, it wasn't even thought about. The first time I met her, she told me about her daily work collecting water for the family and wood for the fire and grass for the buffalo. It took up all her daylight hours, she said. Everything she collected went into her *doko* which was then strapped to her head via a *namlo* and then carried (all 30 kg of it) across the mountains to her mud house. In fact, it was such hard work that a break for her was to come over to our house and cut the grass with me instead of on the hillside. It was almost pleasant, she said, swinging the sickle back and forth across our terraces and chatting to me in Nepali. I had looked at her small frame, as well as the sun setting over the Himalayas, and wondered how she managed day in and day out. Had she ever had a holiday? Had she ever taken time off? Did she long for it? Did she have a word for leisure?

The lack of leisure was a strange concept back then but that day in Canberra, watching the black swans move across Lake

Burley Griffin, the presence of leisure seemed even stranger. We were clearly enjoying it but it felt strange. It was as if I was caught in the middle of both worlds, struggling to reconcile them and not really identifying with either. I wondered whether I could just stay on the outside and watch for a bit longer.

Then I remembered a conversation I'd had with Linda in Fiji.

'I think it takes at least a year to move through transition,' she said. 'It's almost like a bereavement. You need to go through the full cycle of the seasons again to get used to them, to know what to expect and how to respond well.'

'Mmm,' I agreed. 'Maybe the hardest thing for me is feeling surprised all the time, or like an outsider, or a foreigner in a world that I don't understand but I'm supposed to know.'

The black swans moved further away across the lake and I thought about Nepal, where we had actually been the foreigners. We did almost everything wrong but we were expected to. It was embarrassing, but we always had a good excuse. We were foreigners, we were *bideshis*, we were the people with pale skin and funny names who were expected to do everything wrong, so nobody thought it was strange . . . or that we should know how to speak correctly. In fact, they were surprised on the odd occasions when we did! But now we were back in Australia and we were expected to know. Not only did we *look* like we should fit in but everyone assumed that we'd know what to do because it was our home country.

But in the early months of our time in Australia, there were so many things I didn't know. Do parents normally allow their 11-year-olds to go to the shops on their own to buy things? (I knew they did in Nepal, but I had never parented an older child in Australia.) And if you have friends over for meals, can you cook the same thing every time they come? (Especially if it's *dal bhat*?) And what do you wear to a fortieth birthday party, or even worse, a book launch? (If I was in Nepal I'd pull out my favourite purple *kurta surwal* and *chappals* and I wouldn't even think about it.) But in Australia there were too many options and questions and possibilities – too many chances to get it wrong. Even choosing a hot drink at a coffee shop was exhausting, or trying to quieten the voice in my head that critiqued the degree of choice. It felt like I was using up far too much energy being surprised and second-guessing everything and trying to appear 'normal'.

The next day we went to visit my 97-year-old grandmother in her unit at the retirement village in Canberra. As she opened the door I looked down. She seemed so much smaller. I leaned down to kiss her and noticed that her hair was longer, giving her a girlish look. She wasn't using a stick or a walker. She invited us over to the table where she had spread a cloth and placed bowls of grapes, chocolate biscuits and lemon biscuits. The china teacups with the pink flowers were already waiting, but she apologised for the lack of cheese scones. 'I do all my own cooking but I don't bake any more,' she explained.

Then she began to fill the teacups slowly, telling us about the classes in English literature she was doing at the university.

'They're really very good, but this year I might not be able to continue unless they put a loop in. I don't like to sit for an hour and a half and not be able to hear what the lecturer says,' she explained.

We sympathised.

Then she told us about her book club and poetry readings. She reads thirty books a year and writes all her own essays, although somebody else types them for her.

'But now I only read for two hours at a time. My eyes are getting dry.'

We asked about her friends and she described them in terms of how long ago they had died.

Grandma exists in a world that isn't always easy. She doesn't know anyone in Australia who is her age. She can't hear very well and she's often the outsider. In every group she joins she's at least twenty years older than the person next to her. But she keeps going. She doesn't really expect to be the insider.

Perhaps I shouldn't either, I thought. Later that night, we went back to our tent and I searched for the word 'alien' in my Bible. The first reference was very comforting, 'The LORD watches over the alien and sustains the fatherless and the widow' (Psalm 146:9). It was lovely. The Lord knows what it means to be an outsider and he cares for those who don't belong, whoever they are and wherever they are. But the second reference was even more comforting, in a confronting sort of way. In 1 Peter 1 and 2, Peter addresses his entire audience as 'strangers in the world' (1 Peter 1:1). That's what they were. They were a people who had been scattered, who didn't expect to be insiders anywhere. They were living throughout Pontus, Galatia, Cappadocia, Asia and Bithynia but Peter reminded them that they were a chosen people, they belonged to God (1 Peter 2:9) and he urged them *as* 'aliens and strangers' (1 Peter 2:11) to live such good lives (wherever they were) – that God would be glorified.

Oh Lord, teach us your ways. Remind us of what we all are – aliens and strangers. Remind us that it's normal to be the outsider – that we should expect it. Remind us that Jesus was the outsider and he never said that we would be defined by our ability to fit in or our sense of acceptance or understanding, or our talent for making cheese scones. Instead, the Bible talks about being strangers and aliens.

And Lord, we thank you that despite being maker of thought, creator of wisdom and Lord of heaven, you didn't stay there or hold on to it. You sent your Son and stepped into our world, walking around in the dust and the crowds, knowing sleepless nights, tired flesh and aching bones. And even as Jesus spoke to the crowds on the Galilean hills under a hot sun, he wasn't always known or understood or respected. He didn't expect to be.

So Lord, today, when we feel surprised by being the outsider or by a myriad of choices or misunderstandings or falling in between two worlds or not belonging anywhere, help us to comprehend the fact that you have walked our road and felt our pain and suffered for us, so that every day, here, we belong to you and that's enough. Lord, be glorified in all we do and are, today. And remind us that there will come a day when we will never be outsiders again.

Lord, thank you.

Amen

8

SITTING STILL

Something else happened in January that was rather lovely. Our pastor was going away on holiday and he asked me if I wanted to lead the chapel service down at Nepean Hospital while he was away. He explained to me that it ran every Sunday at 11 a.m. and it was open to staff, patients, relatives and anyone else who happened to be at the hospital.

'It's not very long and you don't have to share very much; there's no singing and there probably won't be many people there. But it can be helpful.' Then he apologised for his last phrase which had sounded a bit like an afterthought.

'Don't worry,' I replied, 'you had me as soon as you said hospital.'

I like hospitals almost as much as I like airports and libraries. A lot! I'm not sure whether it's the years I've spent working in them, or the familiarity and the community I associate them with, or whether it's just the extremes of emotion I find there – the living and waiting and healing and weeping and dying. There never seems to be anything in between. I remember graduating in August and within a month I'd seen a lady give birth to twins and then I'd seen a patient die. His name was Brad and he had cystic fibrosis. His face went completely white and his body just stopped. He was 21 and so was I. Afterwards, I stumbled to the hospital chapel and sat there weeping and reading Job.

So if there was a hospital chapel service to be held and led, then I would say yes, always.

The third Sunday in January arrived and I drove down to Penrith early. I wanted to stay calm, to set up my CD player and have time to pray. So I parked, walked past the Intensive Care Unit and then turned left into the chapel. The door was wide open. The light was shining through the stained glass window at the front of the room. There was an old man sitting at the back. He was hunched over with his head bowed and his eyes closed. I tiptoed; I didn't want to disturb him. What if he wanted to be alone? Then he looked up and saw me, so I didn't have a choice, I went over to him.

'Hello,' I whispered. 'I'm Naomi and I'm leading the service today.'

'What?' he said. 'There's a service today?'

'Well, yes,' I said, still quietly, 'in half an hour.' Then I paused and thought I should say something more deliberate or helpful, or even more spiritual. 'Is there something you would like me to pray about for you later in the service?'

'No . . . I don't think so,' he said. 'I need to go to another hospital and have dialysis.' Then he turned his head and looked back towards the door. 'But I'm terrified.'

I sat down next to him and stayed quiet. He showed me his forearms. They were covered in needle marks and bruises and sticking plaster and the smell of the antiseptic trolley. I noticed that he was shaking. We just sat together for a long time and then I got up quietly and turned on some nice music. He thanked me.

Then a lady walked in. She had a long skirt on. I welcomed her and smiled. She told me that she was visiting her mother who was a patient in the neurology ward. Her mother was dying. Then she started crying. 'I've never told my mum that I love her, all these years . . . and now she's dying and I might not get another chance.' I sat down again and prayed for her mum.

Then another lady came in. She told me that her son had been shot and was on the orthopaedic ward. I looked at her and momentarily wondered which country I was in. But then I told myself that I wasn't there to ask questions, I was there to 'be'. So I walked to the front of the room and announced that we would begin the service as it was 11 a.m. I prayed and thanked God that we were in that place, at that moment. As I opened my eyes I saw that one more person had come in to the room. That made five of us.

I explained to them all that I couldn't sing or play an instrument (which was true) but I did have a nice song on the CD player called, 'To Be In Your Presence'. The song reminded me that when life is sad or difficult or dark, sometimes the only thing we can do is sit in the presence of God, be still and be reminded that he loves us. I pressed play.

> To be in your presence, to sit at your feet,
> Where your love surrounds me, and makes me complete.
>
> This is my desire, O Lord, this is my desire.
> This is my desire, O Lord, this is my desire.
>
> To rest in your presence, not rushing away;
> To cherish each moment, here I would stay.

Taken from the song 'To Be in Your Presence' by Noel Richards
Copyright © 1991 Thankyou Music

The song finished and I introduced myself again, in case they'd forgotten. I told them that in the past I had worked at the hospital as a physiotherapist and I'd also been a patient there, and so had my husband and our three sons. Between our stints in and out of Nepean hospital I had also worked in Nepal with a medical mission for six years. And one of the things that being in Nepal had taught me was to be still, to watch the world go by and to sit in the presence of God. In fact, one day a friend of ours had met a very old Nepali lady in an isolated village in the Himalayas. There wasn't anyone else or anything else nearby, so our friend asked the lady, 'What do you do all day long in a place like this?'

The old lady looked at him and said, 'I sit still and let the Lord love me.'

'And that's what we're going to do today,' I said to the four people. 'We're going to sit still and let the Lord love us.'

I read Jeremiah 31:3 quietly: 'I have loved you with an everlasting love; I have drawn you with loving-kindness,' and I spoke very quietly about how God doesn't say to us that he's loved us with a love that wears out, or that gets weary of the loving as we get harder to love. He doesn't say to us that he's loved us with a love that turns away and ignores us when we get sick or when we argue or complain or cry. He says that he's loved us with an everlasting love. That means forever. That means today.

Then I read Isaiah 41:9–10:

> I took you from the ends of the earth, from its farthest corners I called you. I said, 'You are my servant'; I have chosen you and have not rejected you. So do not fear, for I am with you; do not be dismayed for I am your God. I will strengthen you and help you; I will uphold you with my righteous right hand.

I marvelled at the fact that God doesn't say to us that we became his by accident or through a muddled-up oversight on a busy evening. He doesn't say to us that there were names in hats and some of them fell out on to the floor by mistake. He says to us that he chose us and he called us from the furthest corners of the earth. Somehow, before the beginning of time he saw us, he looked into our eyes and singled us out. And even now, in the hospital, he speaks our names quietly and reminds us that he'll strengthen us, help us and uphold us for everything that is to come.

Then I read some more, this time Isaiah 43:1–5:

> Fear not, for I have redeemed you; I have summoned you by name; you are mine. When you pass through the waters, I will be with you; and when you pass through the rivers, they will not sweep over you. When you walk through the fire, you will not be burned; the flames will not set you ablaze. For I am the LORD, your God, the Holy One of Israel, your Saviour; I give Egypt for your ransom, Cush and Seba in your stead. Since you are precious and honoured in my sight, and because I love you, I will give men in exchange for you, and people in exchange for your life. Do not be afraid, for I am with you.

I smiled. God doesn't tell us that we'll walk a journey without rivers, without fire, without fear or without floods. He says to us that when these things come he will be with us; he will not let them sweep over us; he will not let them set us ablaze. We are so precious and honoured in his sight that he gave his one and only son in exchange for our lives.

And then, lastly, I read John 14:27 and 16:24,33:

> Peace I leave with you; my peace I give you. I do not give to you as the world gives. Do not let your hearts be troubled and do not be afraid . . . Ask and you will receive, and your joy will be complete . . . I have told you these things, so that in me you may have peace. In this world you will have trouble. But take heart! I have overcome the world.

And I shared with them that God doesn't tell us that he'll take away trouble and he doesn't promise he'll take away frightening situations. He says that within the trouble he'll give us peace . . . although it might not be the kind of peace we expect.

It might not be like the sunset at the beach or the absence of worry. It will be deep and quiet and unexplainable, and it will come from him, the one who has overcome the world.

They were all quiet: the man with the bruised forearms, the woman visiting her mother, the woman visiting her son and the man in the hospital uniform. There was a lovely peace in the room. I played one more song and then I prayed for all of us, specifically for courage, for healing and for the words to say to the people we love. Then I sat down.

For a long time they didn't leave; they just stayed and sat quietly. I played more music. They said it was the nicest service they'd ever been to. I agreed with them, but not in a smug kind of way as if I'd had anything to do with it. I just agreed in a thankful way. Perhaps, I thought, there's something about worship within pain and fear and weeping that sets it apart entirely. It makes it feel more sacred.

Lord, thank you for opportunities to be still and to sit in your presence and love you. Help us to use them. Help us to be quiet when we need to be quiet and to speak when we need to speak. And even today, as we sit in hospitals and libraries and offices and airports, as we face frightening procedures and unknown tomorrows, Lord help us.

Remind us again of your love for us: a love so ancient that it existed before the human language that would try to describe it; a love so far-sighted that you had us in mind before you sorted out the stars; a love so giving that you would never turn away from us; a love so timeless that as we sit here now, you can't wait to show us heaven; a love so patient, that you will wait and you will count every day until your people have turned back to you, until your people are ready for the streets of gold.

And Lord, thank you that today we can sit here quietly in your presence and in the peace that you give us, which is nothing like the peace the world gives. We thank you and we ask that you'd help us to be still – and let you love us.

Amen

9

THE BIRTH CANAL

The next month (February 2007), Jeremy started big school. He said he was fine. We made his lunch and walked to school, and he reached across and wrapped his hand around mine so tightly that I started to think about my blood flow. We weren't hopping. I held on during the walk but then fifteen minutes later I had to leave him at his classroom, noticing that he'd found his name tag and was busy chewing on his brand new collar. I waved until he disappeared from view and then I went to the swimming pool and did laps with a friend from church – lots of laps. I had a shower at the pool, all by myself. I noticed how easy it was to wash my hair without simultaneously needing to keep an eye on a small child. Then I spent the rest of the day thinking about him and wishing I had a collar to chew on.

But it quickly became normal. We had three boys in school, all of them happy, none of them needing coercion or bribery to finish their page of story writing. So I started running. I walked with them to school around 8.45 a.m. each morning (or whenever we'd found the right number of hats and home-work books) and then I ran a loop up to the next village, across the railway line and back. Millie came too. She soon figured out the best smelly trees and telegraph poles along the way and I soon figured out the best worship songs to play on my MP3 player to get me through 40 minutes of hard slog. Gradually, my feet started to really enjoy the pavement. I noticed it in about April. There was something very lovely about the rhythm of my legs, the air on my face and the tactile nature of my shoes on the ground and the way my thoughts kept time with it all. Somehow it added to my sense of home, as did the purple salvia – which also began to bloom in April.

The next week as we were driving to tennis I pointed out part of my route to the boys. 'Look, that's the path where I run. It's my pavement!'

They weren't all that interested (or impressed) but I realised something had changed in me. I kept watching it out of the car window from a different angle and realised that, for me, the laying down of new tactile memories is important. The physical act of moving through an environment, either running or walking, makes it feel more familiar or home-like than merely driving through it in a car or flying over it in an aeroplane. I was feeling it regularly beneath my feet and it helped.

It also helped with my day. It meant that I had an extra 40 minutes to sing and pray as I ran. It allowed me to think and reflect and get my perspective right before anything else happened in the day. It gave me the discipline I needed – time spent with God out of conscious decision, rather than out of dire necessity, as I had done in Nepal. And of course I realised slowly that whatever country I was in, I needed God's perspective desperately, regardless of whether my outer circumstances were pushing me to the edge or not. I needed it as daily and as regularly as I needed Weet-Bix and *dahi* and a cup of tea and a biscuit. How do I define dire necessity anyway? Maybe in Australia it was just far more subtle.

In April I also had a phone call from my publisher asking me about cover ideas and titles and book blurbs and author bios. It was all very new. I'd never really thought beyond the 65,000 words. We talked for a while and then she asked me about print runs. That was an even stranger question. I'd written the manuscript without thinking it was a book, so I still didn't imagine that anyone would want to read it. I can't remember what I said to her, except that maybe 200 copies would be nice. If 200 people bought it and read it, then we'd be doing really well. It was a nice number and it should be OK because that's how many friends and relations I had . . . and most of them didn't have a choice – they had to read it!

So I was anticipating 200 copies, but even that figure made me nervous. I started chewing on anything I could find and wishing that I could run away and hide somewhere. I noticed that there were some very nice properties for sale further west of the Blue Mountains – they were so remote that they weren't even accessible by road.

'Maybe we could buy one of those?' I said to Darren one night as we hid under the elephant bedspread.

'Not just now,' he said, thinking I was joking.

That same week I'd agreed on a title with Ark House Press but my anxiety continued. What if Darren was right? What if nobody else wanted to read it? What if it wasn't a book? And it was all about our lives! What if people didn't like it? What if they didn't like me? What if they didn't like what I wrote? What if I had revealed too much? What if they thought I was a naïve, navel-gazing dreamer? And what if I was? . . .

One day I caught a train into the city and had an hour and a half with nothing to do except feel nervous. So, to help, I pulled out a piece of paper and wrote down all the awful things that people could possibly think about me after having read the book. I won't tell you what was on the list, except that it was long! Then I read the list from top to bottom and then again from bottom to top and it didn't help at all. I felt worse. So I decided I needed another piece of paper. I found one in my bag and wrote at the very top, 'Yes . . . but maybe one person will be encouraged to know God and love him more because of reading my book.' Then I stared at the second piece of paper in my left hand and the long list in my right hand and I thought, OK, I've got two hands, I can do this.

In hindsight, it was good that I faced the list before publication. As I write this, 25,000 copies have been sold . . . which merely amounts to a lot of people thinking a lot of things. And yes, initially, I did feel very exposed.

The three days before the official release date and launch were the worst. I felt as if I'd gone into labour but my baby was stuck somewhere in the birth canal. *My Seventh Monsoon* was at the printers. Any minute now it would come out and I wouldn't be able to stop it. I couldn't turn back. I couldn't control it. I couldn't do anything. What if I was about to be eaten by wolves?

Then my author copies arrived from the printers. They were still warm. We handled them carefully and took photos. Dennis came over and took a video. It was all very exciting. I opened one of the copies and tried to stay excited when I read some of the sentences. I tried not to squirm and feel enormous amounts of self-doubt. The boys opened another copy and tried to find their names inside. They were quickly successful but then they started arguing about whose name appeared first. I watched them argue and thought about how strange it was that seeing our names in print had somehow made us feel like we actually existed, that we weren't pretending any more.

That night, I was due to attend a women's meeting in Springwood, so I took copies of my books with me and lots of people lined up at the table behind me wanting to buy them and pay money for them. I felt like saying, 'Are you sure? Are you really sure?'

The strangest thing was that they weren't my friends. They weren't even relations. I didn't know who they were. The following week we held a book launch in our church hall, which turned out to be quite enjoyable but after that the numbers of strangers around me increased. They were at the door, sending emails, on the phone, at the shops – all of them wanting to say thank you for the book. They were glad that I had written it.

A month later, I was sitting happily in church, glancing across at Darren's Nepali Bible and thinking about whether I was on the morning tea roster or not. It turned out that I wasn't, but during morning tea, a lovely young couple came up to me and introduced themselves. They hadn't been to our church before but they'd come that day because they'd bought my book and noticed that on the back cover it said which church we attended. They wanted to say hello. Then they took another sip of their instant coffee and said, 'We wanted you to know that we're up to chapter nine in your life and we've been really encouraged by it.'

I stopped drinking my tea for a moment. Oddly, I couldn't even remember what chapter nine was about. I tried to visualise the contents page and wondered whether they were reading about my miscarriages or our renovation or Darren's serious heart condition. I couldn't remember. What were they up to in my life? What sentence were they in the middle of?

I can't remember how the conversation ended but it did leave me feeling slightly more vulnerable and exposed. Of course, I thought it was wonderful that God was using my story to encourage people in their walk with him and to remind them of his purposes through seasons but it still felt strange to realise that there were lots of people, whose names I didn't know, who were up to chapter nine in my life. And that day I went home from church questioning it all again. Why did I do this?

While I was wondering, we all went down to the local park and spent the afternoon chasing Millie around the oval and seeing who could beat her on our bikes. None of us could. She was highly trained and it probably wasn't just a result of our morning runs. Then we went home and had *dal bhat* for dinner, then cleared the table to play Scotland Yard, which had become our next favourite thing after Scrabble. Scotland Yard is a detective game played on a map of London, where everybody chases the thief. The thief remains undercover or hidden for as long as he can – and then he makes a very fast getaway until he finds an even safer hideout. That night, Darren was the thief and he was just as clever at hiding and avoiding and racing away as Millie was.

Later that night, after the boys were in bed and Darren had re-emerged as himself, we talked for a while about the game, avoidance and hiding, racing away, and the things we like to keep hidden or undercover so that we can stay safe and secure and respected and liked. Darren picked up his Bible and read the account of the crucifixion in Matthew's gospel:

> They stripped him and put a scarlet robe on him, and then twisted together a crown of thorns and set it on his head. They put a staff in his right hand and knelt in front of him and mocked him. 'Hail, king of the Jews!' they said. They spat on him, and took the staff and struck him on the head again and again. (Matt. 27:28–30)

I didn't say anything for a very long time. If Jesus didn't run away, if he was prepared to go through torture, mocking, nakedness, beating, rejection, assault and crucifixion that I might be saved and know him and have a real home, then I could probably stop complaining about a little bit of exposure.

Lord, you know what it means to be exposed and beaten and stripped. You know what it means to be mocked and accused of things you didn't do. You know what it means to be spat upon and shamed. You have experienced all these things yet you didn't do a single thing that deserved this treatment. You chose it.

We sit here in our comfortable homes, looking at our pretty gardens and we worry about being exposed and vulnerable. We worry about what people will think of us and what it will do to our reputation. Lord, help us to worry more about your glory and your reputation. Help us to do the things that bring you honour today.

Amen

10

LOOK UP

Five things happened almost immediately after *My Seventh Monsoon* was released. Firstly, I planted a tree (that's how you know you're really at home – you stop planting flowers and you start planting big, proper, genuine trees). So I went to the nursery and chose a beautiful weeping cherry tree with pink blossoms on it that reminded me of the gift of seasons. But because it was mid-winter, the tree looked more like a dead trunk with lots of dead sticks poking out of the top of it. Later that afternoon, Darren came home and asked, 'Why did you plant a dead tree with lots of dead sticks poking out of the top of it outside our bedroom window?'

Secondly, I bought myself a desk. If I was going to be a proper writer and not a physiotherapist, then I would need a desk. That's where they sit, apparently. So I went down to the local second-hand furniture shop and bought myself a lovely wooden desk. It cost me $30 (£20) and it had marks all over it from where previous people had sat behind it and drawn on it. I brought it home, put it in the middle of the living room – the spot with the best view of the gum trees – and I sat there at my desk feeling wonderful.

Then I looked at all the little marks in the wood and I thought about all the other people who had sat at that desk and thought big thoughts. Were we a long line of writers who were connected by a common dream to use words well – to touch people and inspire them? Maybe someone really famous had sat there? Maybe their words had changed lives and the course of history. Before I had a chance to wonder why they'd relinquished their desk, the phone rang, Millie started chewing on the back door to tell me it was 3 p.m. and I noticed that I'd failed to defrost the meat for dinner or put the washing out that morning. So I ignored the phone and the washing machine, collected the dog, ran up to school and decided to leave my big thoughts for the next quiet moment, whenever that might be.

As it turned out, there were a few quiet moments in the weeks ahead, so I embarked on the third big thing – I started writing a sequel to *My Seventh Monsoon*. It felt like quite a leap to presuppose that people would want to read a second book when the first one had only just hit the shelves. It also felt quite presumptuous to write two books that were essentially autobiographies before I'd reached the age of 40. I'd always thought that people who wrote autobiographies were either really old or really famous, or at least really interesting. So in an attempt to hide from the obvious truth that I was none of these and was probably being horribly self-indulgent, I began to call my writing 'devotional storytelling' and then I kept going . . . mainly because I couldn't stop.

But I did find writing the sequel difficult. The problem was that there was already something to live up to. And there was a horrible nagging voice in the left side of my head: How many sequels can you actually recall that are better than the first? How many movies, even in the world of Disney, actually improve as they go on? And how many times do you wonder whether the director is just cashing in on his first big idea? All those things passed through my mind . . . not the cash obviously, but the failure to meet expectations, as well as my own inability to actually write well. The problem was I still had more stories to tell!

I knew I had the stories to tell and many of them poured out as I wrote, but I was also painfully aware that my three journals were at the bottom of Dubbo River. Every time I recalled a moment or a message from our time in Nepal, I knew that I had written better details in the journal. I could even remember the colour of the covers and the page. What did Srijana really say the first time I showed her the vacuum cleaner? Who told me that, as a Hindu, she only prays for the people she loves? What was I doing (and thinking) the day before Jalpa died? It was terribly frustrating (and sad). Fortunately, I'd kept the only page that had floated to the top: 'The mark of any disciple is what it takes to stop him.'

At the same time Darren noticed my frustration and showed me something he'd been reading about William Carey, the great pioneer missionary to India. Apparently, at one point, years into his ministry, a fire had destroyed around twenty of his Bible translations. He had no other copies and no other records of years of work. He must have despaired. But what did he do? He began again. At the end of his life he said, 'Make sure it is recorded that I had no gifts. I just knew how to plod.'

OK, I thought, I'll keep plodding. And slowly it became a blessing. The more I plodded, the more I noticed again the benefit of writing things down and the way that as the words are recorded, my head fills up with more of them. As my head fills up with more of them, my soul sees truths that otherwise would have stayed hidden. It seems that very often we live through times when God teaches us great truth and does amazing things in our lives. We learn and we grow, but we don't always tell the stories to our own family members or even our friends. Maybe we don't even notice the stories. Sometimes we write them in our journal (and lose them) but we don't always take opportunities to use them to publicly point to him. I think we should do that more – give more credit to God. The more I wrote, the more I saw that it was urgent.

The other problem I had while writing the sequel was that I didn't really know how to draw all the stories together. I knew I had lots of them but I didn't know what the big idea was, and that made it hard because the seasons theme in *My Seventh Monsoon* had been very clear to me as well as personally helpful. So I sat at my desk writing about war and poverty, grief and hopelessness, and seeing God's purposes in all of it but I didn't know how to draw it together or how to give God the glory through a disjointed manuscript.

Then one day while I was in the middle of Chapter 11, I caught the train from our home in the Blue Mountains to an Interserve meeting in St Leonards. If you've ever caught the train from Central to North Sydney, you'll know that between Wynyard and North Sydney there's a most spectacular harbour. It sparkles in the sunlight, it glows in the evening, it reflects the colours of the boats and the waterside homes. It is quite beautiful.

But that day, as I craned my head around to see more of the Opera House, I noticed that every other passenger on the train had their head down. One man was replying to a text message, a woman was reading the daily paper and a group of students were fiddling with their iPods, in exactly the same way that they'd fiddled in the tunnel after Town Hall – where there really was nothing to see. I felt like saying to them, 'Hey! Look up. Lift up your heads. It's the most beautiful harbour in the world!'

Now I knew that they'd seen it before; I knew that they probably saw it every day . . . But in a harbour city every day is different: the light and the shade and the colours are different; the birds and the boats and the clouds are different. Look up! I thought. Don't get tired of it. Have a look at the view.

But almost as soon as I had thought it, I realised that I was exactly the same as they were. I was the same with my view as well: my view of the harbour, my view of the trees, my view of the mountains, my view of my family, my view of the gospel and my view of God. I get used to it. I get bored with it. I think I've seen it all before or heard it all before or that I know it too well. I know what they'll say or do (or argue about) and I know what

God will say or do (or remind me of). So instead of looking at the view or at my family or at him, I fix my eyes on the mobile phone, or the ground, or the paper, or the war, or the hopelessness and the mundane life in front of me, missing the majesty of the mountains and the sovereignty of God and the beauty of the people around me who he's made in his image.

The more I thought about it, the more I realised it was the theme for my manuscript, the message for my current season. In every chapter God was teaching me to look up. He was asking me to fix my eyes 'not on what is seen, but on what is unseen' (2 Cor. 4:18). He was showing me that he was still present, even through the war and the earthquake and the death of my friend. He was still active and accomplishing his purposes in Nepal as well as Australia. He was still righteous, fearsome, faithful, everlasting and utterly loving. I just needed to fix my eyes on the extraordinary view, daily. When I sat back down at my desk I typed in the words 'No Ordinary View', and I kept writing.

O Lord, help us today to fix our eyes on the unseen as much as the seen, on the eternal as much as the temporary because we know that we get bogged down in the temporary – in the view in front of us, in the path that we always walk, the train we always catch, the dinner we always make or the conversations we always have.

Sometimes it feels as though this life is a never-ending calendar of things to do – washing to hang out, socks to find, emails to answer and bills to pay – and it's all terribly boring. But even in all of that, you are present. You are at work, you are accomplishing your purposes, you are loving us and revealing yourself to us in every moment, in every train trip, in every new sunrise and conversation, even when we fail to look up or notice it.

So we thank you. And we ask that you'd help us to look up, to see you and your work around us, every day, in every moment.

Amen

11

FINDING THE BALANCE

When *My Seventh Monsoon* was first released, I was initially very self-conscious. I was very aware of the long list in my right hand. But after some months when all the feedback was positive (to my face at least), I began to wonder about it. Maybe God *was* using the book to bring about his purposes in people's lives. It seemed a staggering thought. I even began getting emails from as far afield as Papua New Guinea, Bolivia and England, and they all said the same thing: 'Thank you!'

So then the fourth thing began to happen. I felt the temptation to control it. I wanted to help it along. I wanted to do a thousand things to help get it into people's hands. I've probably always struggled with the balance of trusting and working. On the one hand, I know that God can change people's lives with a few words any time he wants. I know that he can get books published and sold and read by the people he has in mind. But how much help does he want from me? To what degree am I meant to use my gifts and energy to promote and market the work? I know that God can do all things, but it's also true that a book can hide on a shelf if nobody knows it's there.

So by September I was lying in bed at night and coming up with a thousand ideas. Most of them were brilliant, so I started waking Darren up to tell him all about them. He wasn't overly excited, especially by the ones that occurred to me at 3 a.m. (although he was quite surprised by the cherry tree which had suddenly burst forth into blossom outside the window). Most of my ideas were to do with book promotion. Maybe I should ring the Christian bookstore chain and ask about the catalogue or a book signing event? Maybe I could design a website and investigate Christian radio and magazines and women's conferences. And what about—? There were so many ideas that I didn't know where to begin.

Funnily enough, every time I tried to instigate something myself, it fell flat and failed. One of the worst moments was at a book signing at a Christian bookstore near our house. I knew the store well and I knew the manager. The store was big and the opportunity was good. So one day he and I talked about doing a book signing at the busiest time of day on a Saturday morning two months prior to Christmas. It was a very good idea. It was prime time. He ordered extra stock in case the demand was high. He put notices in the window, 'Local author in store, Saturday 20th.' I passed by the window and started to feel excited.

Then the day came. He sat me at a table near the café. There was a pile of my books on the table as well as in front of me. There was a sign. There was even a muffled loud speaker. But nobody paid any attention to it at all. The crowds at 11 a.m. were all in the CD section and the devotional material and the mark-downs. Some of them were even buying Bibles. I tried not to look bothered, because Bibles are wonderful things to buy. Ten minutes later, I thought that maybe I needed to look less obvious. Perhaps authors sitting at desks were scary people to approach. So I picked up one of my books and pretended to read it. I even turned the pages and looked at the words. Still nobody came. I sat there for two hours trying not to look in the slightest bit self-conscious. After about half an hour the staff at the café took pity on me and gave me a hot chocolate to drink at my table. I picked up the spoon and stirred it as slowly as I possibly could. If I could make it last another half an hour it might not look as though I was trying to sell my books at all. It might look like I was just drinking hot chocolate at the café. It was excruciating. Towards the end, a single customer arrived and stood directly in front of me. I looked up. It was Darren. He was smiling but, apparently, he'd almost walked straight past me as well, by accident.

However, the following week I spoke at a church nearby, organised by the pastor's wife. A hundred women came and they bought a hundred books. One of the ladies told me afterwards that she was buying a book for her friend. She'd already read it, and after reading it she had decided not to commit suicide. She had re-found hope in God and his purposes in her life.

Lord, there are so many times when we wonder about the balance. We want to work very hard and we want to trust you – both at the same time. But it's easier to just do our own clever thing. We see the way it should go or the way it would seem best to us, and we try to bring it about ourselves. We do everything we can think of to be clever, but even then, we're not always successful. Instead, we worry, we stay awake all night, we come up with a hundred new questions and solutions and clever ideas. Then, as we watch the ceiling and hear the clock on the bedside table, we realise that no matter how hard we try, we can't even change ourselves, let alone the world.

Yet Lord, within our questions and frustration and ideas we're staggered that we can place all things in your hands, and that's the time we find balance. We can place our worries, our troubles, our fears and our endless ideas in your hands, knowing that your hands are big enough to receive them. Your hands marked off the heavens and measured the depths of the sea. Your hands brought all things into being and caused them to belong to you. Your hands stayed upon your people Israel and carried them out of slavery. Your hands fulfilled every promise that came from your mouth. Your hands were pierced for our transgressions and in that moment brought us salvation. Your hands held ours from that first day when we put our trust in you, and have held them ever since. Your hands bent down, led us and covered us and showed us that, no matter what, we can put our trust in you.

And so today, once again, we ask that you would show us what it means to trust in you and to work for you, both at once. Balanced.

Amen

12

THE WRONG TRAIN

The fifth thing that happened after *My Seventh Monsoon* was released was that I started to get more invitations to speak at various church events and conferences. It was almost as surprising as the emails. One of the early invitations was from a ladies' meeting at a church in Penshurst. Now if you're not from Sydney, I must explain that Penshurst is a fair way to the south of Sydney and it's a long way from the Blue Mountains. The event was a morning tea with a focus on mission and they wanted me to speak about how God was working in Nepal as well as the challenges of missionary re-entry. I could hardly say no. So I organised for Dennis to take the boys to school and I waited for the 8 a.m. train, all geared up for my two-and-a-half-hour train trip to Penshurst. I rehearsed my talk as I kept an eye on my handbag and my laptop and my wheelie bag full of books. The train arrived and the trip began in the ordinary way, except that an hour later the overhead speaker announced that there was a large rail disturbance on the Illawarra line and all passengers were to alight at Central, return to Sydenham and then catch a bus south to Hurstville. So I did that.

The bus was all-stops, at peak hour in the city, so it took a very long time. By the time I arrived at Hurstville I was running an hour late. In Nepal it's OK to be an hour late but in Australia it's not even OK to be five minutes late. So there I was at Hurstville, with my bags, trying to negotiate a large crowd at the bus stop and looking over my shoulder for a timetable. If I could just find the right train, I thought, I might be OK. I could still get there before everyone went home. Penshurst is only one stop after Hurstville. But in the chaos, the electrics had gone down and the timetables were blank. Everyone was milling around and someone shouted that the next train on Platform 1 was going south. So I raced down the stairs with my bags, checked that the platform was number 1 and jumped on the train before the doors closed behind me. There were still no signs anywhere, so I put my bags down and asked someone.

'Excuse me, is this train going south?' I asked.

A lady in the nearest group replied, 'Yes, dear . . . it's the express to Kiama.'

There was a pause. I think I started to moan. I remember leaning my head against the metal pole in the middle of the carriage.

'Is something wrong?' she asked.

I just looked at her. Kiama was two hours away.

'Yes, it's all wrong,' I said, still moaning.

'But it's first stop Sutherland,' she offered, thinking that would help.

It did a bit. Sutherland was still a lot of stations away but it was closer than Kiama. I looked out of the window and could see Penshurst flying past me. I could even see the church.

The lady must have caught my expression because she said, 'Why dear, what's wrong? Where are you going?'

'Well,' I sighed, 'I'm meant to be going to Penshurst. It's a morning tea and I'm the speaker. I'm giving a talk and they're all waiting for me, lots of them. I'm an hour late already and I can't ring them because I don't have their phone number, and now I'm on the wrong train!'

By then, a larger group of women were listening and offering sympathy and cheerful advice. They had probably already bonded through their own missed appointments.

'Don't worry,' they sympathised. 'Just laugh, you can't do anything else!'

I didn't really feeling like laughing. I was moaning. But then, right in the middle of the advice, another lady turned to me and suggested, 'Well dear, what were you going to speak about at your morning tea?'

'Umm,' I said, wondering how I could avoid the question. I then immediately felt guilty for wanting to avoid the question. 'Well, we worked for a Christian medical mission in Nepal for six years.'

'Really?' said the lady. 'And what was that like?'

'Well, it was amazing,' I replied. 'I was actually going to share some stories of how God is working in Nepal.' The words all came out quite quickly.

'Really?' she said. 'Well dear, why don't you give us the talk on the train then, we're all here . . . you could tell us instead.'

I breathed in and looked at them sitting around me and smiling. The train wasn't stopping anytime soon, so for the next ten minutes I talked to the whole carriage. They asked me questions about Nepal, our work and the church, and I answered them. They asked me questions about God. I answered them. They were interested. Then at Sutherland they all wished me well and I said goodbye and I got off the train. I walked to the other side of the platform, waited for the next train going north and retraced my steps back to Penshurst.

On the way, after I stopped looking at my watch and worrying, I began to realise (stupidly and as if I'd never realised it before) that God's plans aren't mine. He's bigger than I am. He has a plan for the women on the train at Sutherland just as much as he has a plan for the women in the church at Penshurst. He cares for his people equally, regardless of whether they're on the train or in the church building, and he will work out his purposes for their sake and in his time and for their salvation. He's always at work, and within his purposes there's no such thing as the wrong train or the wrong job or the wrong path or the wrong season or the wrong home. He's always at work.

The more I thought about it, the more I realised that if I'd been slightly less fixated on my own Penshurst agenda I might have been more aware of the opportunity that God was preparing for me. Unfortunately, I'd jumped out of bed saying, 'Lord, here I am today, on my way to Penshurst, so please be with me.' If only I'd jumped out of bed saying, 'Lord, here I am today, yours . . . so do with me as you will.'

Of course, I did eventually get to Penshurst. They were still waiting for me and it was OK. Much later in the day I read from 1 Peter 3:15: 'But in your hearts set apart Christ as Lord. Always be prepared to give an answer to everyone who asks you to give the reason for the hope that you have.'

Lord, forgive us for pretending to be so capable, clever and in control that we think we can sort out most of our days and contacts and agendas without you. Forgive us for putting limits around the things we will do for you and the things we won't do for you, or the people we will speak with and the people we won't speak with. Forgive us for our small view of the way you work, as if you can't see any further ahead than we can. Forgive us for our small expectations of the things you might do, as if you can't do any more than we can. Forgive us for building up our own plans and our own timetables one upon the other, until we can hardly see over them and we've forgotten who you are.

You are the Lord of all, the beginning and the end, the maker of the plan and the plan itself. Renew in us all a desire to know you and love you, to remember who you are and what you've done for us, even when the train is late and the people are still waiting in an unreachable location. Remind us of the way you hold all things in your hand, and all moments and all opportunities. Teach us to come to you humbly, with reverence, with quietness, with expectation.

Lord, when we get up tomorrow and as our feet touch the floor, prepare us for the train and the bus, the supermarket, the workplace, the hairdresser and the lady walking her dog. Prepare us for the places you'll take us, the people you'll allow us to meet and the conversations you'll enable us to have, so that we might always be ready to share the hope we have in you. In the name of Jesus.

Amen

13

REPLACING TRUST

By the time we'd been back in Australia for more than a year, it was beginning to feel more normal. I'd stopped expecting power cuts every time I began to work on the laptop and I'd learnt how to use my credit card. I'd figured out how to put petrol in the car and I'd even driven to Braidwood all by myself. I'd begun to catch a new vision for what I might do with my life and, somehow, at the same time I'd stopped analysing the nature of home quite as regularly or as thoroughly. I just got out of bed in the mornings and enjoyed it.

However, there were still moments when Australia surprised me. One of them occurred when we were sitting in the local high school auditorium waiting for Stephen's orientation. It was an important day. Part of our decision to return to Australia at the time that we did was tied up with his need for peers and his readiness for high school. So there was a fair bit invested in the decision as I sat in the auditorium that day, and I was very aware of it.

It was information day, so inside the hall there were hundreds of plastic chairs filled with parents and nervous 12-year-olds, all of them glancing over their shoulders to see if they recognised anyone. I was sitting in my plastic chair and also glancing over my shoulder, but not for the purpose of recognition. I was just interested to be able to watch so many 12-year-olds (and their parents) all in one go. Even though we'd been back in Australia for a year, I still hadn't seen such a large group of Western pre-teenagers. While I was still studying them and their parents, especially the boy whose hair was longer than mine, the principal stood up and welcomed us to orientation day. He aimed his remote clicker at the data projector and began to speak.

'This is what high school is all about,' he said. 'Effort earns success.'

He smiled at us as the words flashed up on the big screen. He told us that if our children tried really hard they would earn themselves a place in society and they would experience excellence and achievement. They would even become leaders in our society. He kept on speaking and assuring us that the outcome of effort is always success. As I sat there listening, I felt quite sure it was exactly the same as every other speech across the country introducing the rigours of high school education. But I was still recovering from Nepal where ten years of civil war had led to a state of emergency, martial law and then a revolution. In my Nepali friends' lives it had led to the bombing of their houses and the abduction of their sons and the closing down of their small businesses. It had led to the disruption and the end of their education – if they had even started it. They had never received qualifications, regardless of the effort they put in.

The more his speech went on, the more uncomfortable I felt . . . because in civil war you can't ever assume anything. Every single day the impossible can happen. Maoists can attack your village. The king can take over the country and call 21 days of daytime curfew. The banks and the airport can close down with a moment's notice, and so can the shops, streets, schools and hospitals. And you never know if they'll open again.

So I sat there looking at the principal, and wondered. Even in Australia, can we really be assured of success? Are there really given outcomes for given inputs? Maybe it's different here, I thought. Maybe there are all sorts of guarantees here that I've forgotten about. And maybe it's right to give motivational speeches to 12-year-olds. But even so, I felt uncomfortable for myself. In motivating 12-year-olds are we just building up a façade of tired words and seeming predictability until *we feel* assured? Will all of these 12-year-olds really succeed in the way we like to define it? And what will that look like if they do?

My uncomfortable questions continued for the next half an hour – pretty much at the same rate as the principal's assurances. But I was mostly questioning myself. What exactly was I putting my trust in as I sat there on a plastic chair in an Australian summer? What was *I* thinking about as the principal promised my child success? Do I also replace the only One I can really trust in with thousands of human solutions?

Two hours later, as I walked back across the paved quadrangle, I realised that my own thought life wasn't any better. Sure, I wasn't necessarily believing the principal or his educational jargon, but I was substituting it with other things. I was walking in the sunshine quietly putting my trust in my son's inherent qualities, intelligence and common sense, all of which he has in abundance. It's easy for me, I thought, to replace my trust in God with all of these other worthy things, and then I just make it look like I'm trusting in him. I'm saying all the right things while the going is good, but what if my son loses (or disregards) his innate qualities? What then? If God is truly good and trustworthy, what promise am I really holding on to for my son? And what promise am I holding on to for my friends in Nepal who have no assurance of the next meal or shelter for the next winter?

It bothered me so much that in the evening I knew I had to turn on the computer and write something. I had to find the safe place to burn, as I had done the year before. So, instead of visiting the budget shop (or the basketball hoop), I sat down at my desk and began to type as fast as I could. And this time, the writing turned into a dramatic monologue from the perspective of Mary's sister, whom I named Joanna. She's only referred to once in the Bible: 'Near the cross of Jesus stood his mother, his mother's sister' (John 19:25), although there are other references to the group of women at the cross. I began to wonder how it was for her, being the sister. Did she believe Mary's story in the beginning about the angel? Did she feel shame at the unwanted pregnancy? Did the family become ostracised because of Mary's actions and words? Did Joanna feel frustration that Mary and Joseph were putting their trust in promises that seemed to her to be flimsy at best or ludicrous at worst? And what did she think about trust and success herself? Did she define it in the ordinary way – in the concrete, tangible way that could be projected on to a high school screen 2,000 years later?

Perhaps she was loud and cynical, I thought, as I wrote. Perhaps her hair was coarse and turning grey and she used to frown and push it back in a fluster. Perhaps her sons were younger than Jesus, and maybe she struggled with comparison. Or maybe she didn't. Maybe she was happy for Mary and tried to support her. But the main question I had was about her faith. Did she find it easily? Did the humiliation of the pregnancy colour her belief? Did she take time to put her trust in Jesus? Did she really believe that he was the Son of God, the promised one, the one who would rescue them? And if she did believe, did she see success when she watched his ministry? Did she define it in that way when she saw him amongst the crowds, at the temple, in the Roman courts, in the garden and on the hill?

By the time Christmas Eve at our church came, I felt like I knew Joanna quite well. This time I put a different scarf over my head and disappeared back into the time when she and her family walked on this earth. But it was different this time. Presenting the story from a viewpoint slightly left of the action seemed to create more angst in me, and in the script. Maybe it reflected more of my own questions. By the time I finished I had travelled the harder, more honest road of faith, the one that requires effort, the one where questions are present and so is doubt . . . and where the shock of the crucifixion is only ever trounced by the moment at the empty tomb. He rose from the dead. He has to be God. I have to believe. And belief leads to trust, because if I trust him at the empty tomb, I trust him everywhere.

Lord, we sit here today and we wonder. Sometimes we're not entirely sure. What if he wasn't your son? What if you didn't raise him from the dead? What if he didn't die . . . or save us? What if someone made it all up and we've been utterly and completely gullible all this time? And then we hear ourselves saying it (or thinking it out loud) and we feel a little bit scared – as if the sky might fall on our heads sometime very soon if we don't take it back.

Then, a moment later, we notice that the sky is still blue and wide and that there is a new space inside us – a gladder space, a more honest and open space – and we breathe out again and know that it's because you are here, listening, knowing, becoming and filling the space and questions inside us.

Lord, we thank you because you are Lord always – even in riots and earthquakes and thunderstorms, even when our children don't perform or get the results we'd hoped for, even when success isn't measured the way we thought it was. Even when the tomb closed over and it looked like the end of everything, you remained sovereign and faithful and Lord. Thank you. Help us to remember today and help us to believe, quietly.

As we sit here, we want your promises to transform our days and what we're putting our trust in, even as we cook and shop and commute and email and sit at high-school orientations and worry about success. Some of us are moving house, or changing jobs, or thinking about the next thing on the list, or about study, or caring for others, or who we've forgotten or neglected. Lord, whatever it might be, and within all of that, remind us that you walk it with us, that your presence is with us and your promise of hope and restoration is for all of us. You define success, and it's not marked by grades or salaries or property acquisition – it's marked by an empty tomb . . . and faith.

So teach us how to wait in faith, to hope and watch and pray.

Amen

14

STOPPING FOR WATER

After Christmas that year we went on holiday to Tasmania. It was our leisure time, after all, so we went to visit John and Margaret who had lived next door to us during our years in Dhulikhel. We packed the car, drove to Melbourne, caught the Spirit of Tasmania across the ocean, got back in the car and drove all the way down to Oyster Cove, south of Hobart. During the entire journey, we told 'John and Margaret' stories.

'Do you remember Margaret's lasagne?' I asked.

'Yes,' replied Stephen, 'with buffalo meat and yak cheese . . . and her Anzac biscuits.'

'With home-made golden syrup,' I added. 'She gave me the recipe.'

'And do you remember the day Pepper (our rooster) escaped into John's garden and dug up all his potatoes?' laughed Stephen. We all laughed. We could almost hear the carfuffle that particular moment had created.

'And do you remember the way John would start singing at fellowship?' Darren began to mimic John's brilliantly deep voice, and we couldn't help ourselves, we joined in.

Then we arrived in Oyster Cove and smelt the lasagne straight away. It was just as good, even with real Australian beef. After dinner, we sat with them on their new porch and stared at their new view. In the distance was a blue-green cove. In front of us was a paddock with sprinklers and sheep. To the right of us were boxes of petunias, marigolds and pansies. To the left of us was a tyre swing that John had built for his granddaughters. We all realised that it was quite a long way from Nepal. There were no Himalayas. They drove a car and had a generator for the fire hose. But inside the house were all the same pictures and ornaments that we remembered from their home in Nepal.

And John and Margaret were just the same. They still had morning prayers on their front porch. They still went for morning walks. They still ate lasagne. They still made deliberate relationships with their neighbours. They missed their friends and community in Nepal but they carried on. They were now supporting a little church in Oyster Cove as well as one on Bruny Island. John preached (and sang) and Margaret taught in Sunday school. They drank tea with their neighbours. It wasn't the Dhulikhel ridge – it was different in many ways – but there was more about their lives that was the same than was different.

We drank more tea and ate more apple cake and I started to see how important that was. The things that are central stay the same, no matter how many times we move house or country. But then, staring at the blue-green cove, I wondered . . . would someone say the same thing about us? Were we in essence the same regardless of the country?

The next morning, the boys slept in and I went for a run along their dirt road in Oyster Cove. It was sandy and inviting and perfect for a run. The sun was just making its way onto the water. I ran down the hill and up again. I ran past a farm of long-haired llamas. I ran past interesting houses and native gardens and I tried to imagine living there. I wondered how it would be to make a transition to Tasmania. Then my MP3 started playing the Mercy Me song 'On My Way to You' which talks about God finishing the work he has started in me, so I kept running and sang along with it. I even went as far as the

Our home in Dhulikhel,
Nepal

Our home in the Blue Mountains,
Australia

Too much choice

At the park

Millie

Fiji

Presenting Mary remembers

Our new cherry tree in springtime

Book signing

The main street in Sulaimaniyah,
Northern Iraq

Naomi with Shokhan

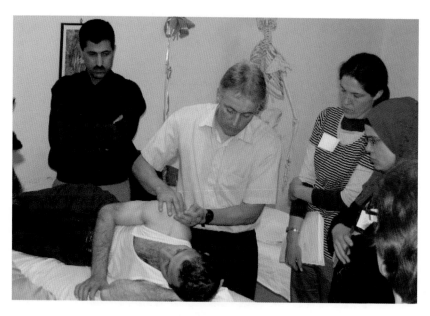

Darren teaching the physios
in Northern Iraq

**The tomb on Easter Saturday,
in Northern Iraq**

Bruce at the mixing desk

Naomi in the linen cupboard

Holidays!

next village. By then, I was still singing (and puffing) but I was thinking mostly about the work – the life, the living and the witness. What had God started in me that he wanted to finish? And how did my destination affect the way I spent my days in Australia?

Just prior to Christmas I had finished the second draft of *No Ordinary View*. It was OK. It wasn't perfect but it was the best that I could do. Sometimes you just have to know when to stop. *My Seventh Monsoon* was still selling well. I had also, in my spare time, collated some of the research that I had carried out in Nepal about personality and mission. The next step was to put that together and form a book for cross-cultural workers, to help them understand themselves and their fellow workers. The publisher had agreed on a title, *Over My Shoulder*.

As I ran towards the next village, praying about what God was doing in me and what he wanted to finish, it was as if I could see a garden in front of me. In the garden there were three trees. They were all quite large and I knew they represented the books I had already worked on. And around each of the trees there were flowers and grass and smaller shrubs. But there was also a large space in the middle, just sitting there, ready for planting. And the more I ran and prayed, the more I knew what I had to do.

Performing the drama at Christmas through Joanna's eyes had been wonderful. Afterwards I had spoken to my writer friend on the phone. I'd asked her how she was and then told her how I was.

'Actually,' I said, 'writing those monologues and performing them has been one of the most enjoyable things I've done in my life.'

There was a pause on the other end of the phone. She was probably wondering how I could be so expansive. So I clarified myself. 'Well not my *whole* life – I mean, I love being married to

Darren and I adore the boys – but I think it's the most enjoyable thing I've done in my *writing* life,' I said. 'In fact, I think that if I could just do *that* for the rest of my life, I'd be happy. I'd never get tired of it.'

It was a fairly sweeping statement but as I ran along the sandy road in Oyster Cove it seemed to make sense. Maybe it had been a natural progression. I'd written my own story, twice. Then I'd written the stories of my fellow workers in Nepal. Then I'd carried that first-person narrative to the Bible. And I loved being able to reflect on the tangible reality of another place and time – the time when Jesus walked on this earth – and to really consider what Mary and her sister might have been feeling.

I arrived back at John and Margaret's house, turned off my MP3 player and sat down on the porch seat next to Darren.

'I know what I'm going to do!' I said, trying not to sound too dramatic. 'I'm going to write my way through the entire Bible using first-person narrative. I'm going to tell the *whole* story. I'm going to start at Genesis and then I'm going to keep going until I get to Pentecost and I'm going to tell the whole thing through the voices of women!' I looked at him, smiling my biggest smile.

'Yeah?' he replied.

We arrived back home from our trip to Tasmania and I sat down at my desk and opened the laptop straight away. I created a new file and called it *The Promise*. I stared at the blank screen, then I wrote down the subtitle, 'The Message of the Bible Through the Voices of Women' and then I wrote down the next heading, 'Chapter 1: Noah's Wife'. It was almost as if I was racing in a triathlon. I'd just finished the bike leg and now I was off on my run. I hadn't even stopped for water.

But there was a problem. And this is a confession. I'd never actually read the Bible all the way through, from beginning to end – although I'd wanted to. Ever since I'd become a

Christian at 12 years old in high school, I'd wanted to read the Old Testament from start to finish. And every year I'd make another New Year's resolution to read it all the way through, then I'd get to Leviticus, or sometimes even worse, Exodus, and then I'd start to think about all the things I'd rather be doing . . . and I'd give up and go back to the New Testament, which was lovely and familiar and all about Jesus. It's not that I didn't know the stories of the Old Testament. I did. I knew all about Daniel, Jonah, Moses, Joseph, Noah, Jacob and Esther, and I knew a lot of truth and prophecies and psalms, but it was a bit like they were all floating around in my head rather than hanging anywhere in a line. And so every year, for almost thirty years, I'd make another New Year's resolution and then I'd get stuck in Leviticus again.

So there we were back at home with the laptop open, and Darren continued his 'Yeah?' conversation. He said, 'Do you know what you could do? You could go and study Old Testament at Bible college. You might find it helpful. It might help you to read the Old Testament all the way through. You never know.' He tried not to point out that he had already studied Old Testament at Bible college and that he'd found it wonderfully helpful.

The trouble with Darren is that he's very clever and he's almost always right. At first, I resist him. I think, surely he can't know everything. And then he does. The blank screen kept staring at me for two weeks and then I gave in and enrolled in Old Testament at Sydney Missionary Bible College. It was the same college that I had studied at sixteen years earlier, before we left for India. It was the same college that Darren had studied at ten years earlier, while we were having more children. They even found my old student number. And Darren was right. My screen filled up so quickly with words and stories that I couldn't type fast enough. It was almost as if someone else was dictating and I was taking the words down. It was as if I'd stopped for water.

I loved it. I never even thought about stopping reading (or typing) at Leviticus! I wanted to find out what happened. I wanted to read the rest of the story (and I wanted to *tell* the rest of the story). The Bible is a narrative. I began to see that for all of those thirty years I'd known that Jesus was the answer but I'd never fully known what the question was or what the problem was. And because I'd never fully understood the problem, I'd never been on my knees with amazement over God's response and the gift of his son. I spent that entire year on my knees in amazement.

Lord, we thank you for your word. We thank you for the privilege of reading it and knowing it and for the way it quenches our thirst and shows us what you're like. For you are holy, worthy, time-unlimited, space-defining, maker of thought, lover of our souls. You've been the same for thousands of generations and civilizations and you're the same even now in this place. We find this almost impossible to imagine. We think we can imagine it, but we can't really.

Please remind us today . . . give us a bigger perspective of time and narrative. Show us that you've been holy and faithful and good for a very long time – and that you will remain holy and faithful and good for an endless time. And as we think about it, please remind us that we're on our way to you . . . that our lives are not just random events here as we get lost in some kind of maze, but they're a deliberate journey to you. Please help us to think about the difference that makes today.

Show us the work you want to finish in each of us – the work of changing and moulding and preparing. Help us to be ready for the work, and to welcome it – the work you have already begun in us.

Help us to not take your gifts lightly or your grace lightly or your friendship lightly, as if it's no bigger deal than turning on the engine, or walking through the supermarket door, or feeding the dog. Let us never have that 'entitled' attitude that makes light of what you've done for us, that makes light of your faithfulness, your grace, your forgiveness and your patience or assumes that it cost you nothing or that it's our right.

Lord, help us to honour you rightly – give you the honour that's fit for your name.

Amen

15

COMPARISON

The problem was, though, that life got too busy. It was probably inevitable. Combining study, assignments, parenting, speaking, writing, managing a home, loving a husband and all those other wonderful (and time-consuming) things can be a challenge. In fact, they're always a challenge, no matter what season or country you're in. During 2008, the contrast with my previous season in Nepal, in the rain, and our early transition period when I was wondering what to do in Australia became so great that one day I was thinking back nostalgically to our seventh monsoon in Nepal and I said to Darren, 'Honey, wouldn't it be lovely to be stuck inside a house for 120 days in a row?'

But there were no curfews in Australia, or monsoons, so every day that year I went outside the house. I went to Bible college, the boys' schools, numerous churches for speaking engagements, the airport six times to go and speak interstate, and I even went to Foxtel studios to be interviewed on TV. During the moments that I did manage to sit at my desk, I had no time to listen to the cicadas, or daydream about paddy fields, or wonder why the boys' bedroom smelt like old soccer gear and popcorn. I prepared *No Ordinary View* for publishing in May, then I re-worked *Over My Shoulder* and submitted it to the publisher. I wrote talks for churches and conferences and high school assemblies. Fortunately, whenever I turned to my fourth manuscript, *The Promise*, it seemed to fall out all by itself, the words tumbling over each other in their haste to get on the page.

One day in April, I was up to Leah. Both Noah's wife and Sarah had finished speaking and they had told their stories quite easily. They were all about covenants and trusting God and what it meant for them to be in relationship with Yahweh. But Leah seemed harder somehow. She was the other wife of Jacob – the unloved one, the wife with the weak eyes. And for me to write her well I needed to pursue thoughts of comparison and jealousy, and the fear (or reality) of being unloved. I don't normally go there. It's too awful, so I avoid it whenever I can. But when Leah spoke through the narrative of Genesis 29 – 35, her voice seemed strained and she went there significantly. The more I read Genesis, the more I identified with her. It was probably that nobody had ever really treasured her or loved her. Maybe she'd spent her whole life being compared to her beautiful sister Rachel (the one with the shining eyes) and she'd always come second – firstly in her father's eyes and then, even worse, in her husband's eyes.

I don't have a sister, so I can't fully imagine it, but I have a lot of female friends – and most of them have shining eyes. Some of them are loud and persuasive and beautiful, and others are wise and reflective and gracious. Actually, most of them are all of those things at once. It's a funny thing (and I don't know if you do this) but if I'm standing next to the stylish ones, I immediately become more aware of my jeans and old T-shirt. Or if I'm spending time with my friend who is perfectly made up, I immediately become more aware of my smudgy eyeliner – which is really only there because I failed to remove it last night. And then of course the more elegant and graceful they are in their movements, the more likely I am to trip over the carpet. In fact, just after reading the Genesis narrative, I went to my friend's dinner party and I sat next to another friend who I hadn't seen for twenty years. She happened to be elegant and intelligent and spoke in the clearest and most articulate voice about politics and religion in the Middle East. At first I tried to sit up straighter and eat more elegantly. Then I thought about my vowel sounds and wondered whether I should say something insightful about the revolution in Nepal (because that was the only political situation that I knew anything about). But the more I worried about it, the more I said ridiculous things.

Comparison is a tricky thing. I think I try to pretend that I don't do it, but then I do it, daily, usually subconsciously. The next week I went to church and our pastor (appropriately) spoke about envy. He said that most often we're envious of the people close to us, or the people who are doing what we want to do, not the stars in Hollywood or even Amy Grant. We don't waste our envy energy on the unattainable, we waste it on our sisters or best friends or the ones who are getting the attention (or love) that we want to get. 'Nahhh,' I thought to myself, remembering that the friend at the dinner party had also told me about her lucrative publishing deal with Bantam Books – she was even paid in advance!

But there I was back at my desk, imagining Leah. Every day she would have watched Jacob loving Rachel. She probably even heard them through the thin walls. No wonder she got upset and ranted in the wheat fields (Genesis 30:15) – what else could she do? And how did she keep going? How did she not drown in her resentment and bitterness? I couldn't imagine it but I kept reading Genesis and then I paused while God had mercy on her and gave her children. That must have been nice, I thought. But did he give her something else as well? Did he give her the grace to keep going? Did he show her that he'd made her different on purpose?

I didn't know but I hoped so. It was the same lesson that had driven me to write *Over My Shoulder* – to show (myself as well as the readers) that we are a body, that we're all different, and that therefore cross-cultural service will look different and be different for all of us. We don't have to be the same or think that there's a model, even if the person down our street has already read the entire Bible in Nepali, is friends with every-one in the bazaar and is already learning Urdu, just in case. God has made us different on purpose so that he can work his purposes to the ends of the earth for the sake of his glory and his gospel.

But even though I know that quite well and I quote 1 Corinthians 12 regularly to myself (and I write about it), I still have so many moments when I glance over my shoulder and notice that other person in our church, or on the mission field, or down the street who has all the gifts that I don't have and I wish I could be like them . . . because maybe then I'd be more loved and articulate and everything would be better.

During 2008, I noticed that the busier I was, the more I fell into the comparison trap. The more I went out of the house to Bible college and speaking events, the less I could do at our local church and at the boys' school . . . and the guiltier I felt. The less I did locally, the more I watched other mums who still had time to attend morning teas and even bake fancy home-made slices to take with them, and I felt bad. I especially felt bad when I watched one particular friend who always made a slice with three layers on it – shortcake, cherries and chocolate – you know the ones that take all day to make and even then they don't work. And at the same time, someone said to me, 'Why don't you just bring the watermelon?'

And so I sat down and wrote Leah and wondered, why do I do that? Why do I constantly berate myself for falling short of the model? And why am I, as a Christian, always tempted to want to know how I'm doing? Am I used to that in other parts of my life? I stared out of the window and remembered high school and university. It was all about grading. In high school, we had 120 in our year group, and every November I'd come home with a long report to hand over to my mum. Even now, I can still see the lists. English – 67th out of 120, Chemistry – 92nd out of 120. It was all very easy back then to know exactly how I rated (not very well) compared to everyone else. And then I graduated as a physiotherapist and the same thing happened in my work environment. Every year, I'd sit down in a window-less room at the hospital and get an annual work review by my boss. It was terribly nerve-wracking. He would rank me on a scale of 1 to 10 in twenty aspects of my working life. It was sobering . . . but at least when it was over, there were bits of encouragement as well. I'd look at all the rankings and think to myself, oh well, I'm doing OK, my patient rapport is 8 out of 10, that's better than 4.

In the Christian life, we don't ever have a scale to measure up to. We don't have work reviews, reward points, pay rises or grades from 1 to 10 – which is good. But maybe the temptation is to look over our shoulders in order to figure it out. How am I doing as a friend, mother, wife, daughter, small group leader, pastoral carer or a Christian witness? And especially that – how am I doing as a Christian? How am I doing as a child of God? And because there are no work reviews or reward points or pay rises or grades or anything else that tells us whether we're doing OK, we can end up comparing ourselves with someone else who we think is measuring up.

I never admit it out loud of course (not until today) – it's always been very subconscious – but the danger for me is that I slowly, subconsciously think I need to grow into my ideal per-son's image rather than into Christ's image. And that month, reading about Leah and thinking about my lack of home-made slices, hospitality, canteen duty and all those other womanly things that I either couldn't do or didn't have time to do, Leah's story really spoke to me. She was a woman who didn't meas-ure up. She had weak eyes and Rachel had beautiful eyes.

Perhaps Leah couldn't make home-made slices either. And she must have spent all those twenty years wishing she was like Rachel, even assuming that if she was like Rachel, Jacob would really love her. Maybe he would adore her like he adored Rachel.

Then I read Genesis 30. At first, Leah seemed so bitter, resentful and upset that she and Rachel had words in the wheat fields (and I didn't blame them). 'Wasn't it enough that you took away my husband?' she said. But even then, in the middle of all that anguish and desire and bitterness, God was present. He gave more children to Leah and he spoke to Jacob: 'Go back to the land of your fathers and to your relatives, and *I will be with you*' (Gen. 31:3, emphasis mine). And for me, sitting at my desk and seeing my non-productive kitchen out of the corner of my eye, it seemed the answer to everything. It seemed as if that one promise would be enough – for her and for all of us – 'I will be with you'. Nothing else was assured, nothing else was guaranteed – not excellence, not success, not love, not achievement – only the presence of God. The promise kept popping up all the way through Genesis and the rest of the Old Testament. 'I will be with you.' 'I will be with you.' But they must have wondered then *how* would he be with them? And how would they know for sure? And perhaps I wondered it as well. How will I know for sure?

That's why the next promise was so important. Years later, just before Rachel died, God spoke to Jacob again: 'I am God Almighty; be fruitful and increase in number. A nation and a community of nations will come from you, and kings will come from your body' (Gen. 35:11). He was going to bless them. Through all of that pain and comparison, God was doing what he always intended to do – he was going to build a nation from the twelve sons of Jacob – and from one of them the king would come. But none of them knew which son it would be. Jacob didn't know. Leah didn't know. Rachel didn't know. Nobody knew. But we know. We've read ahead. We know the story – we know that Jesus, the Lion of Judah, the Saviour of the world, came from Leah's son, Judah. And because he came, he did away with ratings (and annual reviews) forever. There's nothing we can do to make him love us more. There's nothing we can do to make him love us less. There's no 4 and there's no 10 any more. He already loves us, he already died in our place, and because of that we love him in return. We press on in the place he has us, with the gifts that he's given us and with the resources he's given us, because he's the Lord of all and he loves us and he's with us, today and forever.

Lord, we sit here and say thank you because with you there are no scales any more, there are no scores from 1 to 10, there are no reward points or feedback forms. There's nothing we can do to make you love us more and nothing we can do to make you love us less. You've already loved us. You've already sent your son to do away with scales forever. Thank you.

Please remind us again that your design is good. You've designed each of us fearfully and wonderfully and deliberately, for a purpose. You've given us gifts that are unique and precious and not to be compared with the person next door. And you haven't given them blindly or randomly, with your eyes closed. Instead, you've given them for a purpose, for your kingdom and your glory. Help us to see that and use them and be thankful.

And when we think about the way you've made us, we also thank you that you've put us deliberately in different places. You've taken us into universities, the corporate world, migrant communities, little offices, big schools, busy hospitals, Third-World prisons, playgrounds and soccer fields. Help us in all of those places to honour you with the things we do today, the way we speak to our kids and the way we cut up watermelon and the way we love the people in front of us.

Amen

16

BEING SEEN

The other thing that happened that year was that the boys grew a bit. Stephen went to high school. Chris and Jeremy began to run faster. I could never catch any of them, let alone Millie. And at the same rate as they grew faster, they grew louder. Most days I was quite glad that we were *not* all stuck inside our house for 120 days of rain. Coincidentally, at the same time as they grew louder, our house seemed to grow smaller. It might have had something to do with the kind of games they played.

One day, we were all playing Aussie Rules at a nearby oval. I had no idea what the rules were and it probably wouldn't have helped if I had. At one point, Stephen started running towards Jeremy.

'You can't go out of the lines!' he shouted.

'Yes I can!' Jeremy yelled back, running in circles wherever he pleased and laughing at the rest of them.

That's the kind of interaction that happened every moment at our house, regardless of whether we were at the oval or in the kitchen or the living room or the bathroom. And it was about that time that we decided we needed another room. The combination of two bedrooms and a sunroom was becoming quite difficult for the five of us. Whenever visitors came, Stephen ended up sleeping in the corner of the living room behind my $30 desk, which was a squeeze. But I'm already sounding like I'm justifying myself.

The problem was also that, by that stage, all of our friends and relatives had read *My Seventh Monsoon*. In one of the middle chapters, I vocally tackled the issue of renovating. 'Be careful of your heart,' I wrote. 'Don't become enslaved to the things of this world that will pass away.' And of course, I still agreed with myself (and the chapter), or at least the reasoning and truth behind the chapter. But having written it so vocally meant that whenever we said we were thinking of adding another room, our friends and relatives said, 'What? Haven't you already done that?' 'Didn't you say you were never going to do that again?' 'Are you sure?' 'Are you kidding?' 'Are you sure about your heart?'

Exposure and vulnerability are not the only results of pouring your life out on to the page. You also become accountable. People think they have a responsibility to remind you of all the things you wrote three years ago. And that's a very good thing, usually. Bring on some more accountability! But one of the results was that I felt as if I needed to apologise to everyone, or hide, or get defensive in anticipation.

'Yes, we bought a dog,' I'd say, sheepishly. 'Her name is Millie. Yes, I know that we said we never would. But she's very cute – just look at her ears.'

And then I'd think to myself that at least we hadn't sent our kids to private schools yet (mind you, there's always time). That was another thing we said we would never do.

To cope with the extra accountability and the need to hide, I decided that we would add the extra room without making a big deal about it. We would do it very quietly, without telling our friends. So we contacted a local architect, by email, wanting to stay very professional and wanting to try and avoid the comments of helpful friends. She replied by email and said that, funnily enough, she'd just finished reading *My Seventh Monsoon* that week.

That was the same week that the dentist, the lab technician and the bike shop man also stopped us mid-conversation and said that they'd just finished reading my book. The lab technician had even heard me on the radio. Perhaps I will just put a sign on my head, I thought: 'Don't bother talking to me. Just go home and find out everything you need to know in the book . . . and then remind me of the things I said I wouldn't do and am now doing.' It felt a little bit confronting – as though I'd accidentally walked into the spotlight on a stage and the light was randomly following me around the space, while everyone else was managing to stay cleverly in the shadows.

The Monday after we contacted the architect, I walked up to school with the boys as normal. Millie was pulling ahead of us on her lead. Perhaps she's smelt something, I thought. Then Jeremy looked down at the pavement and said, 'It's very hard to see the ants from way up here.'

Jeremy, at 120 cm tall, was just taller than my waist. I bent down a bit so that I could see the pavement from his perspective.

'Yes,' I replied, 'I can hardly even see the centipedes.'

We kept looking at the pavement for the next five minutes while we walked the last block to school and then we said goodbye at the school gate. I stretched my legs (trying not to feel like a rusty hinge), plugged in my MP3 player and began my run, enjoying the wind in my hair and thinking about the ants. Does my sense that God is 'way up there' lead to the delusion that I'm walking around in my hidden world, only known by the people who have read the book or walked in and out of my life? Have I forgotten who my audience really is? Have I somehow talked myself into thinking that he's too far away or too busy, or that he can't see around corners or know what I'm thinking or care very much either way?

After my run and my shower that morning – and a large pile of mushrooms on toast – I sat down at my desk and began preparing a talk for the following Saturday on Mark chapter 9. I pulled out my Bible and read the chapter while drinking another glass of water and stretching my sore legs. I read all the way down to verse 33. I knew the passage quite well, so I wasn't expecting to be surprised. Jesus was transfigured on the mountain (I tried not to read that bit too quickly), he miraculously healed a boy who had an evil spirit and then he and his disciples arrived in Capernaum and sat down inside a house. It doesn't say whose house they were in, but they were all there inside the house, presumably sitting down and relaxing, when Jesus suddenly said to them, 'What were you arguing about on the road?' It must have caught them off guard. Maybe they tensed or stared at the ground or tried not to catch each other's eyes. Maybe they wanted to hide, like me. Either way, they stayed quiet. They didn't want to tell him, because on the road they'd been arguing about who was the greatest. But the thing I found most interesting that day as I read was the fact that Jesus already knew. He didn't really need to ask. They didn't have to tell him. He already knew what they were arguing about. He already knew every one of their inner motivations, every one of their struggles, every one of their hidden inconsistencies.

And Jesus already knew me. He already knew everything I thought and wondered about and imagined and got prickly about. He already knew every one of my inconsistencies and hypocrisies and defensive replies. I started to wonder whether he had a list of them and whether he said, quite regularly, 'Oh no, number 26 again.' He doesn't have to read my book or listen to me on the radio to realise that my heart is weak and scattered, and prone to distraction and temptation. He knows far more about me than the things I chose to reveal in the book. He also knows far more about me than I know myself or am willing to admit to anyone. He knows what I was arguing about last night. He knows what I was whispering to my friend yesterday at the coffee shop. He knows what I was worrying about at 3 a.m. He knows my inner thoughts, motivations and desires. He reminds me of the things I said and the things I promised. I can't hide anywhere. There's nowhere I can go where he won't know me and where he won't love me.

That year, while the books became more widely read and while our friendly architect, whose name was Wendy, drew us another room, I needed to learn that truth over and over again.

Lord, so often we kid ourselves. We think no one can really see us or know us or hear the murmurings inside our heads. So we walk along happily, talking to ourselves and thinking we're perfectly safe, like the ants. But then someone does overhear us or they remember the things we said and we feel exposed and naked and fragile – seen and heard by the people around us.

Please remind us today that every day we're known by you, seen by you and heard by you. You already know all our hidden inconsistencies and hypocrisies and the things we murmur quietly to ourselves at midnight. You're never too far away or too busy to hear us. You never have to ask what we were arguing about on the road. You already know. But, knowing everything about us, you keep on loving us. You keep on forgiving us and growing us, even when we forget to ask you for forgiveness. You keep working in us, slowly, to change us and prune us and to teach us to trust you. You keep making us more like you – slowly, ever so slowly. We thank you for the way you do that, for the way you reveal yourself to us and grow us into your image – through everything – every acquaintance, decision, chance meeting, conversation and even failure. You're there, knowing.

So Lord, we pray today that you would give us strength to keep going and to keep trusting you, even when we feel exposed and naked.

Amen

17

LIVE AS IF IT MIGHT BE

At the same time as learning what it meant to be known, I was still trying to hide whenever I could. A friend at church helped me to make a website so that I could direct the flow of enquiries away from our home phone (and the front door) to a more measured interaction. Then I approached 40 and Darren asked me whether I would like to have a big party. We had celebrated his fortieth birthday eighteen months earlier with a rather large and chaotic event in our back garden.

'No,' I said, smiling at him and appreciating the suggestion. 'I think I'd rather run away and hide.' So he whisked me away for a romantic weekend in a hidden cottage in the Upper Blue Mountains. We spent the days walking along remote bush tracks and we spent the nights talking about all the things we were not going to broadcast to anyone.

We also spent the weekend catching up on sleep. *No Ordinary View* had been released the week before and I was exhausted. The launch had taken place at the Civic Centre in Springwood and 200 people came. Strangely, I was just as nervous as I had been the year before when *My Seventh Monsoon* was launched, except that it was a different brand of nerves. This time I didn't worry about whether they would like it or hate it or judge me or think my writing was terrible. I just worried that I couldn't measure up to myself – that the readers who had enjoyed *My Seventh Monsoon* would be disappointed, and then I would be disappointed as well. Sometimes, comparison works the other way as well. Instead of comparing ourselves to everyone else, we compare ourselves to a different (more perfect) version of ourselves and that's just as debilitating, because it's just as impossible to achieve.

So after our weekend away, to take my mind off my failures and inadequacies, I went back to my desk and kept writing *The Promise*. I'd already moved from Genesis to Exodus and allowed Miriam (Moses' sister) to tell the story of the plagues and the exodus from Egypt. It was wonderful to walk along with her (and *dance!*) and be in a relationship with Yahweh, and on the way to the Promised Land. But then they were in the wilderness, and that was hard (to write as well as to live) because there weren't any females mentioned in the text by name. So I decided that Joshua must have had a daughter and I told the story from her point of view. But it was still hard. She must have wondered and doubted. She must have caved in to the hopelessness of it all or the fear of it all or the empty view of the endless desert.

I think, having not read the Old Testament from beginning to end before, I had missed out on the absolute holiness of God and the seriousness of sin, which kept the Israelites apart from him. Of all the books in the Bible, Leviticus brought it back to me. Even a rash thought, of which I have many, needed confession and a female lamb or goat as a sin offering (Lev. 5:4–6). That's how serious it was to follow Yahweh! Numbers followed on from Exodus with the terrible results of the Israelites' failure, inadequacy and fear. It felt as if it was my failure, inadequacy and fear. I walked through the dust with Joshua's daughter and tried to imagine 40 years of hopelessness and wandering, watching the bodies perish all around me. I had only just turned 40! It was a very long time. My feet blistered and my head hurt and I longed for a home and a Saviour.

Then, one night as I was recovering from the desert experience, I had a phone call from a very good friend. She spoke slowly and I knew something was wrong. She had just been diagnosed with a malignant lump. She was going to have an operation and begin chemotherapy that week. She was taking time off work and spending it with her family. Her husband was also taking time off work and they were spending it walking on the beach. We were quiet and sad. We talked about her children and about home, both here in Australia and in eternity. We talked about God's sovereignty and plans and what he most wants from us. Faith.

The next day I also found a lump and went straight to the doctors. It wasn't a big lump, but it took six weeks for the medical team to work out whether it was benign or malignant, and it felt like a very long six weeks. I kept talking with my friend and I kept on writing. But I stopped running to the next village and instead I went and sat in coffee shops with Darren. During the days – while he was at work and the boys were at school – I sat at my desk and the words poured out of me. I wrote my way through Joshua, Judges, Ruth, Samuel, Kings and Chronicles. I was back in my triathlon. I was thinking about Rahab, Deborah, Naomi, Hannah, Abigail and the Queen of Sheba and the way they would have told their stories. I was thinking about the incredible promise that popped up in 2 Samuel 7. During the afternoons, I ignored my overworked imagination and played with the boys.

During the nights, I stayed up and talked to Darren about all the things it would mean, either way. Amongst other things, we talked a lot about the season nine years earlier when we had discovered he had a life-threatening heart condition. That had been a hard time for both of us, involving three operations, hospitalisations and fearful possibilities. We were still recovering from the stress of it all. The prognosis had ended up being good, but the process had changed him. At the time, he seemed to stop thinking about the future or worrying about the past. He just lived in the present and made use of every opportunity that came his way.

'How long did it last for . . . that feeling of just being thankful that you were alive?' I asked him one night.

'It never went away,' he said.

I rolled over on to my other side but I didn't go to sleep. I lay there, praying for my friend and thinking and waiting. The second lot of biopsy results were due that week. The more I prayed, the more I realised that I didn't have a clue. How does God decide when our time is up or when our work on earth is finished? Why, in Acts 12:2 was James' work finished but Peter's wasn't? Why did James get a sentence and Peter get years of ministry? But even as I lay there, I knew that the time frame wasn't the biggest thing. There was something more important than the time frame and the work and the diagnosis. It was as if he was saying to me, 'Your work isn't done yet. It's not time yet. But *live as if it might be*, write as if it might be, love as if it might be.'

So I went back to my family and I went back to my desk, and I poured myself into breakfast times and dinner times and, in between, I poured myself into the story. By then I was writing through the voice of Huldah. She's not a well-known female character but she's the prophetess in 2 Kings 22 whose task it was to speak to King Josiah after the Book of the Law was found. It wasn't an easy task. The message she gave from the Lord was one of disaster and exile. But in a way I could understand it. I even agreed with her. Yahweh had been so patient and kind, and his people had been so hopeless. By the middle of Kings and Chronicles I was feeling fed up as well. Just *do* something please, I thought. They're never going to get it right; they're never going to remember who you are! (Then again, neither am I.) So Yahweh did something: 'Because they have forsaken me and burned incense to other gods and provoked me to anger by all the idols their hands have made, my anger will burn against this place and will not be quenched' (2 Kgs 22:17).

It was a serious message, and then just three chapters later the city of Jerusalem fell. But as I sat there and experienced the devastation of the city and smelt the burning of the temple, I kept writing from Huldah's point of view and in time I found myself sitting with her in exile in Babylon and reading with her from the great prophet Isaiah:

> Behold, I will create new heavens and a new earth. The former things will not be remembered, nor will they come to mind. But be glad and rejoice forever in what I will create . . . Never again will there be in it an infant who lives but a few days . . . They will build houses and dwell in them . . . The wolf and the lamb will feed together, and the lion will eat straw like the ox. (Isa. 65:17,18,20,21,25)

It was the promise of forever. It was the very first time it appeared in the Bible and it was stunning. We're meant to be stunned, I thought. We're meant to sit here, silent. We're meant to look around and notice that the world we live in is temporary. It's going to wear out. But there's a time coming when there will be no more disease or failure or fear or sickness or blisters or screaming. There will be no more tears. And the reason it's coming is because the Saviour has already come and taken away the things that kept us forever from Yahweh. I sat at my desk, stunned. In the Bible the very best promise of all time comes straight after the very worst act of destruction of all time. I felt as though I was sitting there, smiling with Huldah. It was the country of our own.

Lord, we don't know how long we have here or what tomorrow will bring. We don't know how much time we have. We pretend we do, but we don't. And while we walk here on this earth, death frightens us. The thought of it worries us. We fear for our children and we wish we could find some better form of guarantee.

But you are Lord of forever. You are preparing a city for us. Jesus faced death and it couldn't hold him down, it couldn't keep him. He rose, walked out of the tomb and now he's seated on the throne forever. And Lord, for that reason we thank you that death no longer has a hold over us. It has no power, no clout, no force at all. Instead we have forever.

And forever is a word that we find so hard to understand – that time which extends beyond the time in front of us – a time when the cars we now drive will have rusted away, our jobs won't be remembered and our superannuation plans will be irrelevant. Please show us again what that means. Help us to long for the day when you will make all things new – when we will be with you, in your home, being before your throne, worshipping you forever. Give us hearts and minds full of what's to come. And Lord, as you do, help us to live well today – as if the time we have today is urgent and fleeting and possibly gone tomorrow.

We pray this in the name of your son, whose death and resurrection made it possible.

Amen

18

WE MIGHT NOT GET ANOTHER CHANCE

The biopsy results were good. There were multiple benign cysts but that was all. I sat on a train on the way home from a speaking engagement in North Sydney and sat quietly with God. I felt humbled and commissioned and strangely silent. I felt as though I should be wise in the way I used my days and wise in the way I used my words. I could hardly even write in my journal. The train carried me gently home and I thought a lot about Huldah and her perspective. Then I thought about Esther and her story. She came next in the narrative, and she was the one who stared death straight in the face in order to free her people. Esther walked a road that involved risk and potential hanging in order to honour her God. She walked it in exile, far away from her home and her people. But she knew *why* she walked it, saying, 'If I perish, I perish' (Esther 4:16b). I sat there on the train and could hardly imagine it. She must have pictured the noose around her neck or felt it's thread on her skin, but even in that moment she was able to trust God – that he had her in that place 'for such a time as this' (v.14b), as he always does.

Wow, I thought. He also has me here in this place for this time, for this purpose, for however long it might be . . . and that's what has to make it home. It was fine to still think about the people on my yellow cardboard, but I was at home because he had put me here. That day, on the train, I said sorry again for losing his perspective and for replacing it with my own. So I got home from North Sydney, wrote out Esther 4:14 on a piece of blue paper and stuck it on my desk where I would read it every day and not forget the message. And then I went back to Esther's story.

The more I thought about each of the women and kept writing from their perspective, the more real they became to me. I could picture their faces and their clothes and their homes. I could smell Esther's perfume and feel the roughness of Huldah's garments. I walked across fields with them and through busy market-places. I got out our Bible atlas and Googled everything I could think of to get more images of scenery and crops and buildings in my mind. I fried up combinations of cumin and cardamom with my *dal* to get the right smells in my brain. Then one day I remarked to Darren how wonderful it would be if we could actually go to the Middle East and walk the paths where they might have walked.

The next day Kathie rang. She was a physio whom we had met at an Interserve conference. She was married to Hama, a Kurdish man, and she had lived and worked in Northern Iraq for many years with Youth With A Mission. They were back in Australia briefly on furlough. She said on the phone that she wanted to come over and 'talk shop'. We thought that meant she would come over and we would compare notes on training physios in Nepal with training physios in Iraq. So we said yes. We invited her over the following Saturday and we boiled the kettle and carried the mugs out on to the back deck and we sat there drinking and chatting. But it only took about five minutes for us to realise that she didn't want to talk shop in the sense we had imagined. She wanted us to *go* to Northern Iraq to work with them. At first I smiled, thinking it was ridiculous. It was quite obvious that we couldn't go. It was a long way from home and we had three boys in school.

'Well, yes,' said Kathie, 'but you could bring the boys with you and do home-school.'

I must have pulled some kind of face. The memories of home-school were still too recent. I didn't have enough chocolate! So then she came up with her next idea.

'You could go without them, just for a short time. Even a few weeks would be so helpful. You could do a short module of training and it would make such a difference to the Kurdish people.'

It turned out that, like Nepal, there was no Bachelor degree course available for physio students in Kurdish Iraq. In Sulaimaniyah, a large city in Northern Iraq, there was a two-year Diploma course but, according to Kathie, the teaching was minimal and the need was great. The physios could do with some specialist training. If Darren could even go and teach a short module it would be of immense value.

We looked at each other. I felt quite stunned. I was so sure that Darren would say it was impossible and we would laugh about it as soon as she had gone. Kathie pulled out her laptop and began showing us some of her photos. They were lovely. She showed us the landscape, the markets and the food, and the physio students dressed in their colourful traditional dress. We looked at them with interest, but it was a very foreign country (and idea) and all I could think about was what we were going to say as soon as she left. Then she packed up her laptop and we said goodbye.

When Kathie had gone I started getting dinner ready. While I turned on the oven, Darren came up behind me and said, 'You know, we could go. There's no reason why not.'

I stared at him. He was serious. And that's one of the things I love about him. His favourite line is, 'We might not get another chance,' and he uses it all the time. It's the answer to almost everything. Shall we go for a bike ride or a bush walk or maybe a trip to the beach or shall we go to Northern Iraq?

Yes, of course we'll go to Northern Iraq . . . we might not get another chance.

So we planned to go for two and a half weeks and during the next few months we booked flights and we booked child-minding (our parents). We looked at the atlas, we read books about Iraq and we felt completely daunted by the whole thought of being in the Middle East. But I also felt amazed. I pored over the Bible atlas even more than before. Abraham and Sarah had walked straight through Northern Iraq on their way to Canaan from Ur of the Chaldees. I would be able to walk where they walked, smell the smells they smelt and feel the ground under my feet, and I would be able to imagine myself being there thousands of years earlier.

I think I was so absorbed by these thoughts that I hardly noticed that it was the end of the year. I finished studying the Old Testament and I took my exam. We celebrated Christmas at school and church and with all of our relatives. I watched the boys receive all their awards at presentation day. I even put a scarf over my head and performed 'Mary' at two different churches. Then I ran out of wrapping paper and I visited the budget shop next to the supermarket. It was the same shop, with the same lights and the same blow-up snowmen and oversized puddings that had so upset me two years earlier, but I hardly noticed it. I just walked inside, bought my paper and walked back outside again. I didn't even think about it. As I walked back through the car park it struck me that I was either fully at home here in Australia or I was so busy anticipating another country that I didn't even notice the red paraphernalia and the strangeness of the West.

There were all sorts of deadlines we needed to reach before we went to Iraq. Darren prepared a unit of teaching on shoulder injuries. Fortunately, he was doing his PhD research on shoulders so that was very helpful. He even found a work colleague who spoke Kurdish, so he prepared a video of shoulder assessment and treatment in the Kurdish language. I kept writing *The Promise*, feverishly. I wanted to finish the manuscript before we left for Iraq.

So I moved through the prophets and Ezra and Nehemiah. I spoke through the voice of a singer who had just returned to Jerusalem from Babylon under Cyrus and then I spoke through the voice of Shallum's daughter. Fortunately for me, she was mentioned in Nehemiah 3:12. Shallum and his daughters repaired the section of the wall adjacent to the Tower of the Ovens. I thought about how it must have been for them. They were back in the Promised Land. They had returned from exile full of anticipation, but then their home wasn't what they imagined it would be. After so many years of talking about it and waiting for it and thinking that it would solve everything, they didn't even like the look of it. They were disappointed in everything: in themselves, in the land, in the concept of home, even in Yahweh.

I breathed in and recognised myself in them. I was just like them – so easily disappointed when life and home didn't measure up to my rather high expectations. Then Haggai arrived and they were cut to the heart, and so was I. It didn't matter where they were, he said, they needed to honour Yahweh. They needed to sing and praise and remember – and so did I. Then I wondered if it had been somehow (and strangely) easier for them while they had been in exile? Was there something about their surroundings and the statues and the treasures of Babylon that caused them to remember the one *true* God, Yahweh? Had it also been somehow strangely easier for me to honour God while we were in Nepal (temporarily) than when we were in Australia? Was there something about my own land that enslaved and reduced me merely because of expectations and complacency? Had I somehow forgotten that my life in Australia was just as temporary as my life in Nepal? I wondered and I kept reading and writing.

I imagined the Israelites grumbling and learning, confessing and longing for something more, for something good, for the time when their hearts would be made pure or somehow washed clean. Haggai reminded them that would happen. Yahweh himself spoke: 'In a little while I will once more shake the heavens and the earth . . . and the desired of all nations will come, and I will fill this house with glory' (Hag. 2:6,7).

That was when I stopped and pictured them working on the wall and collecting figs and replanting the ground, and *anticipating* the fulfilment of God's promise. And I anticipated it as well. Even as I sat at my desk and watched the jacaranda leaves turning golden that summer, I knew that I was not so different to them. Sure, I lived on this side of the cross and the empty tomb. I knew and experienced the work of the Holy Spirit in my life, in a daily and life-changing way. But no matter how much I found purpose and meaning and belonging in my life in Australia, I still longed for the time to come when I wouldn't bounce around like a ping-pong ball with God, from intimacy to distance. I longed for forever. I sat with Shallum's daughter and heard Yahweh's promise that he himself would come to the temple.

It was an incredible promise and it had to be. It had to last for 400 years until the Messiah came. I closed the Old Testament in awe and wonder. I was amazed by God and the extent of his patience with us, his people. I left my Bible sitting on my desk and I deliberately didn't open it for a whole month. I wanted to feel the wait. I wanted to stop and feel the years, the anticipation and the terrible fear that perhaps Yahweh had turned his back and forgotten all about them.

In the meantime it was January, so we took the kids for a holiday to New Zealand. We went to see Maurice and Michelle and their kids, who had lived with us in Nepal. They were on my yellow cardboard picture as well (and so was their home) so I wanted to see them in real life. We stayed with them on the

outskirts of Auckland and reminisced. We talked about the
bus trip to Tansen when everybody threw up. We remembered
eating watermelon at Lakeside just before I gave birth to
Stephen. We remembered the day we walked for two hours to
get to the INF conference through strikes and a daytime curfew, and then the way we all piled into the ambulance to get
home, driving straight through the crowds of soldiers. We
remembered laughing and praying and learning.

But we didn't just reminisce, we started living again and
making new memories. We travelled south from Auckland
and walked through the Tongariro Crossing. We climbed
Ngaurahoe (a dormant volcano) and then we slid down the
scree, leaping and sliding through deep piles of rubble and
stones that lodged themselves in our shoes until they made
sores on our ankles. We laughed at the way it felt like skiing
and flying and crashing all at once. Sometimes there's no way
to describe something so extravagant.

Then we played cards at a holiday shack in Ohakune and I
leant on the windowsill and watched the sheep outside. My
ankles were sore from the stones and my mind was sore from
a year of almost relentless over-activity. I took my weight on
my arms. Outside the window there were hundreds of sheep,
all bunched together on the side of a green hill. Some of them
were lying down on the grass and others were standing, eating. It looked strange to me at first. I couldn't remember seeing sheep lying down in Australia, so I stared at them and
thought that maybe it was because we didn't have enough
green grass in Australia. Then, thinking about the grass
reminded me of dinner, which we ate and enjoyed and then
we settled down in bed to read another chapter of the Narnia
series, followed by Psalm 23.

It was probably the time of day and the extent of our activ-
ity and the year we were recovering from, but the psalm was
perfect bedtime reading. It was all about rest. Even as our eyes

were closing, I knew that it was important. It didn't matter whether we were on holiday, flying down a mountain of scree or feverishly meeting writing and university deadlines – we needed to know how to rest, because God had made us for rest. 'The Lord is my shepherd, I shall not be in want. He makes me lie down in green pastures, he leads me beside quiet waters, he restores my soul' (Ps. 23:1–3a).

Just like the sheep, he wants us to lie down in the green pastures and rest.

Lord, we thank you that you give us opportunities and possibilities and exciting new invitations, but you also give us times of quiet and rest. We pray that you would teach us to rest regularly – not just when we're on holiday but also when we're meeting deadlines and have full schedules. Teach us to be still and notice you and be restored in the midst of our busyness as well as when we're lying beneath the trees . . . because you created us to need rest.

Lord, even as we think about rest, we know that we've gone searching for it in all the wrong places this week. We've tried to find it in chamomile and hot milk and white noise. And we've tried to find it at all the wrong times, forgetting that you've made us for rest in the noisy times as well as the quiet ones. In all of that we've failed to see that the only way we can truly rest and be at home is to find that rest and home in you.

And thank you that as we rest in you, Lord, we find new strength and energy for the day and year ahead. Thank you that you never get too busy to have time for us. You're always with us, you're always reminding us that you love us and restore us. Thank you.

Amen

19

MUD ON THE CARPET

In early February 2009, our church celebrated 50 years of existence. Extra chairs filled the brick foyer, extra people arrived from other states and the temperature reached an all-time high. I can't remember what the actual temperature was, but it must have been high because the elders started handing out bottles of iced water during the church service. Our boys thought it was great. I won't tell you what they did with the bottles of iced water (that's why you have an imagination) but the good news was that nobody passed out during the sermon due to the heat. The visiting speaker spoke about dependence.

He said that when we look back on our lives, we usually remember good times and hard times (and in between times), times when things appeared to be going backwards, as well as forwards. In the five decades of this church's life, he said, there had been both good times and hard times. There had been times when key people left, when the remaining members disagreed and when the money ran out . . . but even in those times, there had been fruitfulness. It had brought about a new dependence on God, a new prayerfulness and humility, and a fresh desire to proclaim the gospel. And that's actually what we want: we want a deepening relationship with Jesus more than we want nice pews and an unremarkable annual general meeting; we want growth in Christ-likeness more than we want Christian veneer and outward politeness; we want humility and dependence and prayerfulness more than we want a smooth path. He said that in the years and months ahead we can probably expect some more of that – hard times as well as good times, humbling times as well as pain-free times – because it will cause us to grow.

Darren and I and the boys walked home from church that day, still trying not to pass out in the heat, and we talked a bit about the things that caused us to grow – the things that forced us to face our insecurities and outward veneer. It was quite a long conversation, as you can imagine.

When we got home we turned on the air-conditioning as fast as we could. We didn't want to face the heat if we didn't have to! The problem is, though, that we never quite know when the metaphorical heat is coming. We don't always get to the air-conditioner quick enough. The next month, in March, *Over My Shoulder* was released, very quietly. There was no great big launch or fanfare or people playing the bagpipes or press releases, which was exactly how I wanted it to be. The book was specifically designed for cross-cultural workers, so I wanted it to slip quietly into their hands – the ones who were walking through their local bazaars and looking over their shoulders at everybody else doing a better job. I wanted them to find it helpful, to read their chapters on personality type and to use those chapters amongst their teams, in their far-flung places. That's what I wanted, but it was one thing for me to want it and another thing for it to actually happen – especially in the beginning.

One Monday afternoon in March, I was sitting at my desk and Googling my name (which I honestly hardly ever do, but it's the only way to find book reviews) and there it was – the first public review of *Over My Shoulder.*

'Oh good,' I said out loud, 'someone's actually read it!'

And then I clicked on the link and began to read the review, which wasn't good at all. The reviewer said that *Over My*

Shoulder was a bit like studying stitching techniques on cricket balls – in other words, it was boring and tedious and it wouldn't interest anybody. He then tried to describe what it was about (getting the Myers-Briggs Type Indicator letters wrong) and he concluded that 'some writers have far too much time on their hands.'

What? . . . Too much time on my hands! I stared at the screen, feeling a little bit sick and wondering if I could possibly have read it wrong. Then I started talking loudly to the man inside the computer. 'You think I have too much time on my hands? Do you want to know what I did this morning? Or what I did last year? Or what I did during the *two years* it took me to compile my research and interview 49 people (in the middle of war and rain and home-school)? Have *you* ever lived through a civil war?'

For some strange reason he didn't reply, so I got up from my desk, walked up to school and then drove Jeremy to gymnastics, trying not to shout at anybody as I drove down the highway. Then I sat in the plastic seats at the gymnasium, watching Jeremy hurl himself around the high bar and I pulled out my journal, thinking that perhaps I could talk loudly to some of the blank pages (or even hurl them somewhere). Unfortunately, the page before the blank page had a description of the church service the month before. 'That's actually what we want – a deepening walk with God rather than outward Christian veneer (or outward acclaim),' said the visiting speaker.

Oh dear, I thought, here we go again.

The problem is I'm a writer who wants to be read. I want my words to connect with you and I want us to sit here together and say, 'Aha.' I want us to drink tea together and moan together about the muddle we're in and the questions we can't answer and the holes we keep falling into day after day . . . and then after about a thousand hours of chatting, I want us to catch a glimpse of something very far off, something very tiny on the horizon. It's a light. It's only just flickering, but as we keep chatting it will get a little bit brighter and the space inside our hearts will get a little bit bigger and then we'll suddenly realise that we're going to keep going (with our eyes on the light) until the Maker of the light calls us home. That's what I want. That's why I write today.

But as well as sitting here with you and watching the light, there's a little piece of me that wants to be liked. I want you to like me and I want you to like what I write – because the writing comes out of me. It's my insides. It's all that I have to give.

And that day on the way home from gymnastics, I felt as though someone had walked all over my insides and left mud on the carpet. So I got home, parked the car, sat down next to Darren on the green lounge chair and I told him all about it. He could probably tell anyway by the way my face had gone a paler shade of green, but he was genuinely concerned and he listened to me. Of course, I didn't show him the link to the review (because I couldn't bear to see it again) but I managed to repeat it word for word.

Darren, being lovely and kind, empathised with me. At first he asked, 'Who was the guy anyway?'

'I don't know,' I said. 'But he's horrible.'

Darren laughed. 'Well, maybe he doesn't actually know very much about cross-cultural mission or personality or the great commission and maybe he lives here in Sydney and he goes to Avoca for his holidays and he's not really all that qualified to review your book. Maybe he's not the reader you had in mind. So don't worry about it.'

I smiled.

'Yes I know,' I replied, 'but it still hurts my insides.'

He held my hand.

'It does. And it will keep hurting your insides every time . . . but the thing is that not *everybody* is going to like you, and not everybody is going to like what you write.'

I pulled a face.

'Why can't *everybody* like me?' And then I added (in a quieter voice), 'I wish there was an easier way to grow up and become humble and prayerful.'

'Yes,' he said, 'but we haven't found it yet.'

Oh Lord, we want to grow up, to become more like you, to be made ready for heaven. But so often the process of growing up hurts our insides and it feels as though somebody's walking mud all over our carpet.

And then we sit here and remember your son, who made himself nothing, took on the nature of a servant and became a man – a man who was not always admired or liked or revered or looked up to. He didn't always receive good reviews. He didn't always receive public acclaim or even acknowledgement for who he was. Instead, he humbled himself and became obedient to death – even death on a cross. He took all our shame away and defeated our sin. He was led like a lamb to the slaughter and cut off from the land of the living, so that we, who were full of pride, self-centredness and need, could be given a new peace and a new spirit, so that we could breathe again, believe again and remember who you are and what we're here to do.

Lord, please help us today – give us a fresh desire to honour you, an honest thirst for your word, a longing for your salvation, and a hope that is in you rather than in our own cleverness. Grow us and remind us that you love us. Please show us what you think about achievement, freedom, success and being exalted. And as well as that, show us what you think about worth and home and what it means to be your child. And then Lord, when we're really very quiet, show us what you meant when you said the truth would set us free.

Amen

20

STORIES OF NEED

We set off for Iraq in April 2009. The salvia in our front garden was once again gloriously purple. The snowdrops were popping up beneath the silver birches. I wondered momentarily why I noticed the beautiful things so much more clearly as I was leaving them, rather than when I was living with them. But then I sighed inwardly and didn't answer my question. We packed our bags, waved goodbye to Stephen (who cycled off to school on his bike) and then we took Chris and Jeremy up to school. We tried not to think about what would happen if we didn't come back. We hugged them goodbye and they ran off to play handball. They seemed perfectly fine but we weren't fine at all. We boarded the plane at midday and immediately reached for the closest copies of *The Guardian* for old times' sake and to try to pretend we were OK. As always, the night lasted so long that we not only read the entire newspaper but we also watched four and a half movies.

Finally the sun caught up with us and it began to rise over the Middle East. As the sun rose, we crossed the Arabian Sea. I looked out of my window and could still make out the last piece of land behind us on the west coast of India. Then the Gulf of Oman was up ahead and what had only ever been real in story books and movies and the news was about to become real under our feet. We dropped 10,000 metres and landed in Dubai.

It glittered. We walked around the souk in Old Dubai for nearly three hours. It was full of Indian shops and market stalls. On the one hand, it was terribly foreign, so I paid attention to the smells and detail in new ways. I stared . . . and the first thing I noticed (not that cleverly) was that for every thousand men walking towards us there was one woman. I pulled my scarf and sleeves further down my arms and stayed close to Darren. We stopped to look at watches and scarves and then we saw a boot maker. He sat on the same type of little stool as they always sat on in Nepal. He chatted to us and then he fixed my *chappals* for only three dirham. And as well as being foreign it was also familiar – the clothes and watches and saris and rugs and smells of cinnamon and cloves and samosas. But this was a man's world. I immediately began to compare it with Nepal and wondered where all the women were. In Nepal, the women were valued less than the buffalo, but they were still out there on the streets, cooking and shopping and chatting. In early morning in Old Dubai the women were nowhere to be seen, and neither were the children. It was quite striking. There were no childish voices laughing. There were no children playing.

We caught a taxi to the other side of Dubai and asked the taxi driver where the children were.

'Inside,' he told us.

On our right was Atlantis on the Palm and Jumeirah Beach, where there was a seven-star hotel. We walked between the two landmarks and stared at the high rises built on sand. The taxi driver later told us it had all been constructed in the last ten years. Before that, he said, there was nothing, just sand – desert. And before that? He didn't know. I wondered about their stories, history, memory, home and heritage. Where did the people come from?

We took photos on the beach with Atlantis behind us and thought about how close we were to where Miriam, Moses and Joshua wandered in the desert on their way to the Promised Land. We were so close to the place where they built the tower of Babel – and we thought about the fact that everything eventually crumbles, even the things we build with the greatest of care and with the most advanced materials. It all eventually returns to dust and the sand on which it is built.

That night we got back on an aeroplane and flew to Sulaimaniyah, Northern Iraq. We arrived very late and it was not glittering. The day before we arrived there had been desert storms in Saudi Arabia, so everything was covered in a fine red dust. We were picked up from the airport and driven through a busy city with modern buildings. There were no beggars on the street or shanty towns, like in Kathmandu. There was no obvious need. There were traffic lights and dual carriageways and proper shopping centres lit up in the dark night. I kept comparing it to Nepal, because that was all I knew.

That night we slept well and had bread with sheep's milk yoghurt and green almonds for breakfast. Then we joined Kathie and Hama on the flat roof of their house where the whole city was spread out beneath us, under the dust. On the outskirts of the city there was a ring of mountains and green hills but they were stripped of trees. Hama said there used to be almond trees and apricots and even oaks but Saddam Hussein had banned all agriculture in the 1980s in order to starve the 'Peshmergas', the Kurdish freedom fighters. And then the people didn't need to produce crops. They had oil and they had income, so the most fertile land in the Middle East became bare and barren and would remain bare and barren until somebody needed it. It was a strange thought.

It was Sunday, so that night we drove through the busy city again and went to the International Church. It met in the basement of a room in the city, so we went down two flights of stairs to find it and then sat on black plastic chairs. After some time we stood up to sing 'Mighty to Save', and the whole thing amazed me. Here I was, in what used to be Babylon (almost, but not quite), reading the psalms of David (written prior to the temple being built) and singing about Jesus, who is mighty to save and who fulfilled every promise 2,000 years ago. And there I was, standing with the descendants of Esau, 2,000 years later. The sense of place and history and intersection overwhelmed me, to the point that I couldn't even write about it.

I turned to the girl sitting next to me. She was Iraqi and in her fifth and final year studying medicine. Her family were Christians and they used to live down south in Baghdad but moved to Sulaimaniyah because it was less dangerous. She had been caught in crossfire many times, but once in particular, when two bullets went straight through their car. The seven passengers were not hit, but her cousin and uncle were captured by Saddam and ransomed.

'I always lock the doors now,' she explained. 'And I think about spies. But I'm not scared. This is just how it is. This is home.'

Ah, I thought, later that night. Home is not necessarily safety. It's the place we always go.

The next morning, the shoulder course began. Darren put on his best jacket and began to lecture thirty of the diploma graduates in true Darren style. That meant that by lunchtime they were laughing at his jokes and it was somehow being translated into Kurdish by a wonderful man named Ezzet. I was listening and enjoying it as well but mostly appreciating my back-seat role.

'All you have to do,' Darren told me, 'is help the girls when they need it.'

'Good!' I said.

The girls were lovely. They were dressed in bright colours and pointy shoes and had woollen scarves over their shiny hair. In between finding supraspinatus and the coracoacromial ligament and walking to the anatomy labs and back, a few of them started to chat to me about their lives and their work. Eventually, we talked about 1991. I asked them where they were that year and they told me. In 1991 Saddam had bombed Sulaimaniyah and gassed the nearby towns. Two million Kurds escaped into the mountain range towards Iran. They walked there. Most of the girls said they had been just children at the time but they could remember it. They were glad that I asked. Intessar told me that her relatives had stayed and died. Shokhan told me about camping out in the snow on the mountain for months until the Gulf War ended. She told me about being hungry and thirsty and cold. Chra told me about escaping all the way to Iran. They all knew about the 182,000 people who had died and they knew about the 4,500 villages that had been destroyed. Their friends and relatives had died. Their homes had been decimated. They all had a story to tell and they wanted to tell it.

Afterwards, Shokhan turned to me and said, 'You're the very first person who has ever asked me about our story. Thank you.'

A place can be needy without looking needy from the outside. And a place can be home without looking like home from the outside.

Lord, teach us to see people the way you see them, and to hear them the way you hear them. Forgive us for all the times when we've only listened to the people who seem like us or who have stories like our own. Forgive us for thinking that the only real stories are the ones we know and understand. And please remind us that no matter how it looks from the outside, everyone has a story, and some of them are inexpressibly awful. Some stories are so sad that we may never stop crying if we begin to put them into words. You know them all. You know the stories we haven't dared to speak out loud. You know the ones we haven't spoken because no one has ever asked us about them.

You sit here with us, knowing our stories and understanding. Thank you. Help us to be the kind of people that really listen to the people around us, who ask about their stories, who speak when we need to speak and listen when we need to listen.

Lord, when we become overwhelmed by desperate stories or ongoing need, remind us that you see more than we do. You see past doorways and windows and closed shopping centres. You see places and people and hearts, when all we see are tiny marks on the atlas. We thank you that your faithfulness reaches to the places that we struggle to find on an atlas – places like Sulaimaniyah and Erbil and Halabja. Lord, you formed these places and the people who live there. You formed them, you know them intimately and you have been with them all of this time – loving them as well as counting them, naming them and collecting their tears in a bottle. Please Lord, draw them to yourself, show them who you are . . . and let their stories change the way we live today.

Amen

21

EASTER IN IRAQ

Back in the shoulder course, the students were revising. Darren asked them how they would test the length of the upper trapezius muscle. Faruq stood up, answered correctly and then settled back in his seat, smiling. Aram answered a question about shoulder impingement. He called it 'pigment', but we knew what he meant. Then Darren began to teach them about ligament injuries.

'The mechanism of injury,' he explained, 'is often a direct blow to the shoulder. For example, patients might tell you they've fallen out of a tree.'

There was a pause while some of the students looked at each other. The girl in front of me frowned and looked at Ezzet, who was still translating. I looked out of the window. There weren't any trees in Northern Iraq. Perhaps the students had never climbed one? Darren noticed the looks on their faces in time and smiled. He'd probably been thinking of our other Himalayan home, where patients regularly fell out of trees while cutting leaves for their buffalo. He looked over at Ezzet and wondered what the corresponding example was in Iraq – a car accident, a bullet? But Ezzet kept speaking and the lesson continued, in Kurdish.

It was a funny moment but it was also the kind of thing that used to make me hesitant about going short-term to other cultures and thinking we could do anything useful. It was too hard! Without good language or cultural understanding, how could we possibly say useful things, let alone do anything remotely sustainable? What were we thinking? We were kidding ourselves! I leant back on my seat and remembered the thousands of mistakes we'd made in Nepal. Like the day that I had stood on Sita's front doorstep and tried to do business without going inside. She'd been so embarrassed that she had physically manoeuvred me into the house mid-sentence. Then there was the moment when my friend answered, '*Tikcha,*' when I asked her if she wanted a drink. I thought it meant, 'I'm OK, I don't want a cup of tea.' But years later, I realised she'd said, 'Yes, OK, I'd love a drink.' I sighed to myself and rehearsed the countless times I'd worn the wrong things, said the wrong things, done the wrong things, thought the wrong things and generally confused everybody, including myself. And they were just the moments I'd known about. What about all the others? And what were we thinking, coming to Iraq?

At that exact moment, Shokhan turned around to me from the seat in front. She caught my eye and smiled at me. During morning tea she had told me the next part of her story, quietly, so that nobody else could hear. She was pregnant. She had put her tea down, smoothed the scarf over her belly and said that nobody else knew. She wouldn't normally have told me either, but she wanted to tell me because it mattered. It mattered to her that somebody else, from another world and another life knew about her life and her story. And she wanted me to know about not only the hard times in the snow and cold and hunger, but also the current story, of an ordinary Kurdish woman living and loving and counting the days till she held her child. I relaxed into my chair, smiled back at her and was desperately glad that I had come.

The next day Darren and I went off to the archaeology museum. We moved slowly around the building, staring at pottery and implements and necklaces that had been dug up from the local area. In one large pot there were the bones of a woman, dated 4000 BC. It could have been Noah's wife. There were large urns from the Neolithic period, statues from the Babylonians and a freeze of King Ashurbanipal. I felt as though I was walking my way through the Old Testament instead of reading it. Underneath my feet and in front of my eyes it became something tangible and visual and three-dimensional. It had smells and colours and shapes as well as words. I pulled my journal out of my bag and sat down on the steps, writing as fast as I could, trying to keep the images in my head for as long as I could.

The next day was Easter Saturday, so we piled into Hama's pickup and drove out of Sulaimaniyah, past the hills and surrounding villages into the landscape in which so many of the Bible stories were lived. We saw fields covered with yellow flowers and the occasional red poppy. We saw shepherds in long coats, grazing their sheep. We saw boys on donkeys and men carrying piles of firewood. We got out of the car and felt the ground beneath our feet. At one point we walked across a field and up some wooden stairs to get to an original tomb, dated 200 BC. It was set in the side of a hill and it was cold and clammy. I felt the damp air on my skin and breathed in the smells and imagined how the women must have felt on that first Easter Saturday morning so many years before.

Just prior to coming to Iraq, I had finished my manuscript of *The Promise*. During January and February, I had deliberately left my Bible sitting still and unopened on my desk. I had felt the 400 years of waiting and the terrible fear that perhaps Yahweh had forgotten them. I had gone about my business but I had almost enjoyed the silence, wanting to feel the pain of abandonment as they had. But then, during March, I had opened it up again, starting at the Gospel of Matthew and as I read the words poured out again through the voices of Mary, Joanna and Mary Magdalene. It was astounding. After thousands of years of an impossibly broken relationship, Yahweh's answer cost him everything he had – his own son. And now I was actually in that place so close to where Rachel and Leah must have married Jacob. I was walking the paths where the Queen of Sheba must have walked on her way to meet King Solomon. I was very near the town of Erbil and others where King Sennacherib had brought the ten northern tribes into exile in 720 BC.

But it was Easter Saturday, and I was mostly thinking about the women as they waited. Their teacher and Messiah, the one who they loved and whose words had touched them like no other, whose hands had healed them and comforted them, had been buried, cold and lifeless and finished, in the tomb. They weren't even waiting for anything. They certainly weren't waiting for Easter Sunday as we know it, they were probably just wailing, so sure that their story (and his story) was finished. They didn't know what was coming.

Then, on the way back to Sulaimaniyah, Kathie asked me if I was currently working on a book. She'd read the other three books and wanted to know if there was anything else she should know about.

'Well, yes,' I said. 'It might sound odd, but I'm writing my way through the Bible . . . using the voices of women.' I paused and tried not to sound too apologetic about it. 'It's actually been wonderful. I started at Genesis, I finished at Pentecost and it's really helped me to put myself in the narrative in a tangible sense and to feel the truth at a deeper level.' Then I pointed out of the window of the pickup, 'And look at this . . . look at these hills and these ridges. This is where they walked!'

We both stared out of the window and tried to imagine the scene thousands of years earlier, in a different century and with people speaking in a different language and obeying the custom of different rulers. After some time I said, 'You know, I can see the women and hear them and imagine what they might have been feeling. I can touch their clothes and imagine their conversation. But do you know what I'd love to do?'

She didn't. Neither did Darren or Hama.

'Record,' I said. 'Record their stories. Read them out loud. Turn the whole thing into an audio book, or something like that, where I could actually capture it more vividly, or more the way it was meant to be.'

It was a stupid thing to say. I didn't know anything about writing, let alone recording an audio book, so as soon as I heard myself say it, I pulled it back in again.

'Of course, that's impossible though. I don't know anything about recording and I don't know anybody who does and I certainly don't know anybody with a studio or gear or anyone who would be remotely interested in recording an audio book for me.'

At that point, Kathie's friend Ruth turned around to me and said, 'Actually there's a guy in the Blue Mountains who could do it for you. He lives around the corner from you and he has a studio and all the gear. He's worked for the Australian Broadcasting Corporation and he's very professional. His wife is an architect. Her name is Wendy.'

'Ah yes,' I said. 'We know her.'

We did. She had finished our plans and submitted them to council before we left for Iraq. But I didn't mention that to Ruth. Then Kathie pointed at the snow-capped Iranian peaks that were just coming into view on our left.

'Ring him when you get home,' advised Ruth.

'OK,' I replied, 'I will.'

We kept driving back to Sulaimaniyah and on the way we stopped at a field on a hill belonging to Hama's closest friends. They were digging the soil, ready to plant flowers and vegetables. We hopped out of the vehicle and Darren reached for a pick, wanting to help them. I sat on a smooth rock nearby and watched them for a while. The sun sank low in the sky and cast shadows over the grass and the road beneath us. I could hear the trucks. It was the same road on which two million Kurds had fled from Saddam to the mountains in 1991.

Kathie showed me how to find thistles in the fields and how to skin them and boil the roots to make a snack. We ate them for afternoon tea as the sun set behind the mountains and the fields turned golden. Then we got back in the car and drove back, reaching Sulaimaniyah as the lights were coming on and the evening calls to prayer marked the end of another day.

The Christian presence in Northern Iraq is very small. On Easter Sunday we went back to the International Church where there was a small but colourful gathering in the upstairs section of the basement. Most of the people were wearing trad-itional dress. I looked through the windows at the streetscape and was struck again by where I was. Yahweh began his work in this very place; he spoke to Abraham right here with his plan for the nations. This is where it all began, but where is the witness now? Why is it so small? And why did we need an Esau anyway? Surely it would have been better if he had just worked on Jacob?

We sang again. The message was based on John 20 and 21. Jesus rose again, he walked out of the tomb. Later he met his disciples on the beach and said, 'Feed my lambs.' We're the lambs. And the reason we needed an Esau was so that we could have a choice – so that we could choose which way to walk. We can choose to follow the shepherd or not. We can scuttle off down the hill or along the highway, or we can choose to stay and listen to the one who calls our name. Today, wherever we are, we can choose to love him, not because we have to, not because it was obvious or necessary or the only viable solution, but we can choose to love him because we can, because he allowed us the choice.

After the service, Darren spoke to a local man who had escaped Sulaimaniyah in 1999 and become a Christian while he was a refugee in England. At the same time as he fled, he developed an inoperable bowel cancer and lost 20 kilograms. At first he went to every doctor he could find in the UK and prayed to every god he could think of. Then one night he watched a movie about vampires and noticed that the devil was scared of the cross, and he wanted to know why the devil would be scared of a cross? Wouldn't the devil be scared of God? Why would God be in a cross? So he asked his friend and his friend told him that there was a man called Jesus, thought to be God, who was killed on a cross. That night, the Kurdish man went home, tied two sticks together, put them on his wall and said, 'OK God, I'm no longer a Muslim. I'm a Christian. Show me yourself.'

Several nights later he had a vision of Jesus. The sky opened up for two minutes and he saw Jesus, risen from the dead and at the right hand of God. He believed. And he was healed of his bowel cancer. He returned to Iraq and he spoke to 100,000 people about what God had done for him.

Sometimes the witness occurs in ways we can't see or know or understand or even vaguely fathom. Sometimes the witness occurs in vampire movies.

Lord, we thank you that you bring about the witness, that even while we sit here and find it impossible to imagine how you will do it, you still reveal yourself. You make yourself known: in barren fields, Iranian mountains, desert sandstorms and you even use vampire movies to speak to people. Thank you that you call your people by name, that you make yourself known to them through visions and stories, through conversations and the reading of your word.

Thank you, too, that the grief of Easter Saturday didn't last forever – it came to an end and you rose from the dead. Lord, help us to be stunned, to on occasions feel so sad and starved of your presence that we begin to really feel what the resurrection meant – for them, for us, for now, forever.

And when we do go through our equivalent of Easter Saturdays, those hard times when we think you're silent or that you've turned your back on us or are too busy for our problems, please remind us that you've already done it – you've already risen, you've already saved us, you've already forgiven us. We've heard it many times before but we need to hear it again, because for moments only we understand grace and we say thank you – and then we quickly forget and move back into trying to make you love us more. We're so sorry.

Amen

22

RUNNING SLOWLY

During our second week in Iraq Darren visited hospitals and medical centres with the physiotherapy graduates. He got up early and drove all over the city, giving seminars and stopping to see patients who had lost limbs or been seriously burnt in the conflict. He saw the reality of life after war.

While he visited patients and talked to groups of medical doctors, I met with four different groups of cross-cultural workers. They all wanted me to present workshops for them using my third book, *Over My Shoulder*. I was worried at first. What if they didn't like it? What if it *was* really tedious, like stitching cricket balls? What if all my examples were from Nepal and it didn't relate to life and struggles and hope in the Middle East?

I shouldn't have worried. In every group we drank sweet Kurdish tea and ate Easter eggs and talked about stress and service and humility. We were honest about the types of situations (and people) that drove us crazy. We shared our ridiculous extroverted stories and our quiet introverted moments. We were surprised at the different ways we viewed the world – some of us saw the minute detail and others enormous possibilities. We got teary when we shared the moments that were beautiful and worthwhile, and when we genuinely appreciated and complemented each other. Above all, we realised that, although we have different personalities and ways of looking at things, deep down we were all essentially the same.

It didn't matter whether we held a Dutch, German, American or Brazilian passport; it didn't matter whether we spoke Kurdish, English, Nepali or a strange combination of all three; it didn't matter whether we wore saris, trousers or *jili kurdis*. We were all made in the image of God and we were made to work together as his body, for the sake of his kingdom. That week, I realised that my 'body of Christ' (and my home) was getting larger and larger with each passing day.

The night before we left Iraq there was another desert storm in Saudi Arabia. We woke up and could hardly see out of the windows. They were covered in a thick layer of red dust. Kathie was already up and cleaning them, while Hama was on the roof checking the generator. We finished our last breakfast of bread with sheep's milk yoghurt and green almonds and joined Kathie at the window. For some reason we started talking about the blue and yellow paint job.

'It's very nice,' I commented, 'underneath the dust.'

'Yes,' she smiled. 'It is.'

Then Hama came down the stairs and joined us. 'For so many years,' he told us, 'we didn't paint our houses at all and we didn't renovate them. What was the point, when we knew there would be bullets in them or Saddam would bring the bulldozers in? And he did. So there were bullets in the walls – all of them – for as long as we could remember. But now here we are: for the very first time we're painting our walls, we're making a home, we're really living. We didn't think it would ever be possible.' How wonderful, I thought. Home is a place where you can paint the windowsills.

Darren and I carried our bags downstairs, said goodbye to Kathie and Hama in their beautifully painted home and made our way back to ours on the other side of the Arabian Sea and the Indian Ocean. It turned out to be an equally beautiful home, filled with three excited boys and an equally excited dog, who jumped all over us in wild delight.

It was lovely to be home and it was lovely to be hugged and to catch up on all their news. It took hours. We unpacked our bags and showed them the new rug and pictures. We told them some of our stories and we heard about their time at Grandma's. None of the boys had sustained any broken bones on the new rope swings and ladder. Stephen had made new bike tracks. And Millie hadn't escaped or gone to chase kangaroos, so that was wonderful as well.

It was lovely to be back, but the transition seemed quite sudden. I felt like one of those dolls that you can turn the head all the way around and the arms and legs move in opposite directions and then you laugh at it because it can still walk somehow. I walked over to the supermarket, trying to keep my legs and head going in the same direction. I saw a lady walking towards me in shorts and I tried not to stare at her knees. Did she realise how much skin she was revealing? Then we all went down to the local oval and watched the boys' weekend football games. The oval was surrounded by trees waving in the breeze; it was filled with children playing and laughing.

One of the other dads had heard we'd been away somewhere.

'You've been on a holiday?' he asked.

'Yeah, kind of,' Darren replied. 'To Iraq.'

The man just looked at him.

'You went to Iraq for a holiday?'

We hadn't really, but the funny thing was that it felt as though we had. We'd had a wonderful time. We'd made new friends and visited new places and heard some ordinary, some atrocious and some beautiful stories. We'd walked their walk for a very short time and it would significantly change the way we prayed and thought about the Middle East. It wasn't just a place on a map any more or a two-minute spiel on the news. It was a real place, with real people who had real names like

Ezzet, Intessar, Faruq and Shokhan. They were painting their windowsills, thinking about their babies, treating their patients and making their homes, just like we were. It's a shared walk, wherever we are.

A week later, while I was still adjusting, I rang Wendy.

'This is not about the house plans,' I said, in preparation. 'They're fine. They're very good in fact. But we've just come back from a wonderful trip to Iraq and I have another idea.'

I told her about my idea for an audio book. She put me on to her husband, whose name was Bruce.

'Yes, I have a studio. Yes, you can record in it. Yes, I have the gear. Yes, I have lots of ideas and no, it's not a funny question at all.'

Two weeks later, my friend Mel and I turned up at their front door. I was terrified. So was Mel. She had heard me mention *The Promise* at church the week before and volunteered her services. At that stage we thought it would probably take about two days to record the book (because that's how long it would take to read it), but I knew I would definitely need another reader and she was keen. I couldn't quite believe that I was a reader myself, let alone that I needed another reader.

The studio was separate to the house but it was connected via the linen cupboard. We walked into the main room and noticed that Bruce had some very calm music playing. It didn't help. We looked at the sound desk and then he opened the door to the linen cupboard and showed us how it all worked. Inside the linen cupboard there was a music stand and some smaller equipment with leads and headphones and microphones.

'So, if we leave the towel cupboard open like this we get a perfect sound,' he explained.

'Ah . . .' I noted, not getting it at all. In the main section of the studio there was a stripy lounge chair, as well as the mixing desk and his computer and speakers. Mel and I sank into it and didn't know what to say next.

He looked at us.

'So, what are we going to do today?' he asked.

'Um, we thought we'd try to record Leah and Joanna,' I explained.

'Sure,' he agreed, looking down at the script. 'Who wants to go first?'

Neither of us!

In the end, Mel (being very perceptive) noticed that I was shaking like a paddy field in August and volunteered to go first. She went into the linen cupboard, put the headphones on and read Leah. The chapter starts off with a sentence that reads, 'I do know what it's like to have a sister.' And from the very first line, Mel became Leah. I sat in the lounge chair and listened to her. She made me cry. She read the words exactly as I had imagined them – probably even better. Every so often Bruce asked her to stop and repeat something.

'And again, from the start of the paragraph,' he said.

She paused, slightly changed the emphasis or pronounced something more clearly and, usually, it worked. A couple of times we all re-considered the emotion behind the lines – and then she gave more of herself to the argument in the field and the moment when Rachel died. An hour later, she came to the end of the chapter and emerged from the linen cupboard, smiling. We all had a cup of tea. It was great.

Then it was my turn. That wasn't quite as great.

'Your voice is a bit shrill in places,' said Bruce, trying to be objective. 'And a bit fast. Let's start from the top again.'

We did. Numerous times. And it wasn't much better.

'Maybe you need to try slowing down some more. Pause from time to time. I think it's the light and shade in your voice that you're missing – you need some variety, not just constant stress.'

It was about that time that I remembered Bruce had been an audio director at a television station for many years and was now working freelance.

'And use your diaphragm,' he said. 'Or maybe pretend that you're actually talking to someone real . . . not just the bath towels.'

OK, I thought, pretend. Imagine that there's someone lovely in the cupboard with me. I looked around me at the 1-metre-square space and couldn't quite see where they'd fit but I pretended as well as I could for another two hours. It didn't work. We got to the end of the chapter and I could tell he wasn't happy. It might have been the way he sunk his head into his hands. After another try, I came back out of the linen cupboard and we had another cup of English Breakfast tea.

'Maybe speaking is not your strength,' offered Bruce helpfully.

I looked down at my cup of tea and stayed quiet. I didn't tell him that in the previous three years I'd done 182 speaking engagements and had daily requests for more. I just finished my cup of tea and tried again.

It was better, but it wasn't good enough.

'Well, basically,' he said, 'you're a 7 out of 10 and you need to be a 9.'

That was when I sank into the chair. It was hopeless. It felt like my work reviews and book reviews and yearly reports all over again. It was like an assessment out of 100 and a comparison with 120. It was like reward points and grading and pay rises. It was too hard. I'd never be good enough.

So I said goodbye and left the studio, then went home and cleaned the house. I took a bag of old clothes to the recycling bin. I ran Millie around the yard and jumped on the trampoline. Then I walked up to school and met the boys. It happened to be the same week that they were training for their athletics carnival at school, so we ran down the street instead of looking for centipedes.

Then Jeremy turned to me and said, 'Mum, did you ever go in running races when you were little?'

'Yes Jem, I did,' I said. 'Why?'

'Well, when you got to the end of the race, did you ever think that maybe you could have run faster, that you hadn't really run your fastest?'

I paused for a bit before I answered . . . 'Yes Jem, I think I always felt like that.'

I told him about being in primary school at West Epping where I always ran against a girl named Susan. She had very blonde hair and she ran very fast. Every single year and in every single race, I came second to her. I even remembered the feel of the grass afterwards as I collected my red ribbon and wondered whether I could have run faster. Could I have stuck my neck out a bit more or taken off a bit better or hurled myself into the straight? Could I have done it? Had I done my very best?

I didn't know then and I didn't know now. Was Bruce right? Could I speak better? Could I use my diaphragm more and be a 9? I didn't think so, but I still agreed with his emphasis. He wanted the best possible product so that people would listen to the audio book and hear the message. He wanted them to be moved by the truth of the gospel and the astounding love of God. He didn't want them to be distracted by my croaky voice or weak diaphragm, so I needed to be a 9. I agreed with him completely. I just didn't know if I could be anything more than a 7.

So I went to bed worrying and then phoned him the next day. We decided to send the demo to the publisher anyway to see what they thought. After all, it was their decision as they were funding the project – and it was only a demo.

They liked it! The next week I met them at a coffee shop in Chatswood and we talked about the whole project. We made a budget and we discussed various voices and CD duplicators and cover options. It was very exciting.

But then we had to go back to the studio and actually record. I had to face my weaknesses. Sometimes having wonderful ideas is much more fun than actually carrying them out.

Lord, we're all a bit hopeless. Some days we wake up and our legs are weak, our eyes are tired, our necks hurt and our voices are shrill and scratchy. We can't speak well, write well, paint well, sing well, cook well or do anything well at all. We're just 7s. We want to do things that honour you and speak of you, but often we don't feel as if we can. We don't even know how to do that. We keep coming up with new ideas, but they're not always great and they don't always work, then we feel generally hopeless and wish we'd stayed in bed – or some-where else a long way away, like Iraq.

Lord, on those days lead us gently. Pick us up and put us back on the path, and remind us that the path is yours and that you're the author of new ideas – you give them to us. Reassure us that you'll do something in the middle of our hopelessness – you'll provide what we need. You don't always just use our 'personal best' times. You don't say, 'Oh dear, that was more than fifteen seconds, I can't do anything with that run', or 'That set of sentences was too shrill, I can't use that.' You keep moulding us and changing us and using us – even our slow, stumbling runs that probably could have been a lot faster and our shaky voices.

So Lord, help us today to keep walking forwards, or keep speaking, or keep writing, or keep recording, or keep singing, or keep working, or keep parenting . . . or keep doing whatever it is that causes us to shake and tremble with nerves, but that brings honour to you.

Amen

23

READ IT FOR GRANDMA

I'm weak. I'm a broken pot and I have a broken voice. I can't use my diaphragm very well. Some days I can't even put two words together well. But I'm also very good at avoiding those kinds of realities. So, for the next three months, I searched among my friends and listened to their voices and concentrated on the way they spoke. Maybe if I could find enough good voices to cover the other characters, I wouldn't have to face my own hopelessness? So I prayed about each of my twenty characters and wondered which of my friends' voices would suit each of them. I stopped thinking about myself.

We started with Mel again. She had passed the test the first time around (and enjoyed it!) so we turned up at the studio again and she read Rahab.

Of all the characters that I had written about, Rahab was one of my favourites. I found her story so profound. It seemed as if God looked at that whole city of Jericho – with maybe a couple of thousand inhabitants – and he looked for the filthiest, most rejected, degraded scrap of humanity he could find . . . and his eyes fell on Rahab, the harlot. It felt as though God said to me, 'Now see what I can do with someone whose heart is responsive to me.' She was clearly a harlot, she'd given herself indiscriminately to men – lots and lots of them – and she probably wasn't proud of it. She probably didn't choose this way of life or enjoy being a social outcast and treated as just a body – someone given monetary value only, never respect. So maybe she spoke with an edge to her voice, anger boiling away beneath the surface because she'd been sinned against as much as she had sinned.

Mel went into the studio and started to read the chapter. At first, she sounded just like Leah, so she came out again and we talked about Rahab (and ourselves) some more until there was a hint of contempt and angst in her voice. It was perfect. She went back into the linen cupboard and kept reading. I was struck again by the narrative. More than anything, Rahab's story reveals what God is like. He chooses her and he reveals himself to her, all within that awful story, even as the men waited at the door and the city was destroyed. It was incredible. That's how God works in the hearts of his people and draws them to himself, one by one. He chooses us and shows us who he is and somehow we know him and respond to him. He is the 'God in heaven above and on the earth below' (Josh. 2:11b). All these thousands of years later, on this side of the cross, we see more and know more, but ultimately it's the same. He sees us in the city wall, behind the kitchen bench, at the post office or in the office, and he shows us who he is and rescues us.

After Mel finished Rahab, we moved on to Deborah, the warrior judge. She was very powerful. I could hear the strength in her voice as I wrote the chapter. It was the time of the judges and the Hebrews were in the hill country of Ephraim. I pictured her sitting beneath the palm tree in splendour and listening to her people. They were hopeless. They were in the Promised Land but they were hopeless – they were disobedient and forgetful and weak (just like me). I even recognised the cycle: they'd sin, then cry out to Yahweh and he'd show them mercy, again and again. Each time he'd send someone to bring them back to him, and then they'd do it all over again. In this case, he sent Deborah, the one with the commanding voice, the prophetic gift and the penetrating eyes.

We chose Nat, a friend from church. She was the drama teacher at the local high school, so we thought that if anyone could do it, she could. The two of us turned up at the studio on a Saturday morning and I tried to explain the background to the chapter.

'Well, I think Deborah is incredible,' I said. 'She's unique in biblical history. There they all were in Ephraim, in a mess, and God raised her up deliberately to deliver his people. He probably made her like that on purpose – confident and commanding and powerful.' I tried not to make a contrast with the way I felt he'd made me – insecure and weak and lacking in confidence. 'All the Hebrews knew that, which is why they submitted to her – even Barak, the leader of the Hebrew army.'

'It's amazing how the chapter ends, with her trust in Yahweh and the outward evidence of that trust – the success of the battle,' Nat agreed.

'That's right,' I continued, 'but then sometimes I wonder if there was a flip side to her success? Was she ever tempted to base her identity on the success itself, rather than in Yahweh? Were there ever days when she thought that the victory was the answer, rather than Yahweh himself? And do we ever think that?'

We didn't know, but the three of us talked about success for a while and I said that I felt that I'd never really experienced success, so it was difficult to know, or to relate to Deborah. The other two just looked at me. Bruce raised his eyebrows. The very next week, *No Ordinary View* won 'Australian Christian Book of the Year 2009'.

So we recorded Deborah, and I sat in the lounge chair completely still. The hairs stood up on the back of my neck. Nat read it in such a way that all the words seemed new to me. I didn't even remember writing them. I just stood up on the hill and saw the dust cloud beneath me and heard the noise of the ten thousand men and the nine hundred iron chariots and I saw the glory of Yahweh. It was incredible.

Exactly the same thing happened for all of the other chapters. Margaret came and read Hannah and she was soft and humble and quiet and I could hear her pain as Penninah taunted her. Then Melissa came and read Abigail and she was gracious and queenly and generous and I could smell the roasted grain and the raisin cakes as she rode out through the gorge to meet David. Then Cecily came and read Sarah and she was old and scratchy and controlling in the beginning, and I felt the tears run down her cheeks when Hagar walked past with her child. But in every case, God was good. He provided what the women needed for thousands of years – he provided the grace and the faith and the ability to keep going – even when they couldn't see past the desert or the Babylonian statues or the broken wall. He helped them to wait and to love and to serve while they trusted in his promises, and while he kept his promises. He promised that he would give them a saviour and he promised that he'd make their hearts new.

And every day, the message meant more to me. I kept going back to the studio and I kept thinking about the way God was providing what I needed – the friends and the faith and the ability to keep going – even while I couldn't see past my letterbox or my bushy back garden or my insecurities about my voice. He was still good. He was still doing what he had in mind, even when I couldn't always see it – even when I spent days worrying about my voice. He was still God.

But we also had a deadline. The book launch was set for 16 September, so the finished book files and the audio book needed to be checked and submitted to the publisher by 15 August. Every day during late July and early August I received and answered emails from Ark House Press, checking the covers and the book blurbs and the audio insert and the formatting. Did I like the colours and the font and the images? Were the footnotes correct? Did the subtitle correctly capture the essence of the story? Could I check for widow and orphan lines and hyphenations? By 4 August I was getting more and more nervous. Not only was I worried about the book itself and what people would think of it (and me), but we still hadn't recorded Joanna. I still hadn't faced my fear. By then, we'd done all of the other characters, but I'd avoided my own. So as we lay in bed that night I told Darren how worried I was. What if I couldn't do it? What if my voice was still too shrill and hopeless and my diaphragm was too weak and my reading was too intense and I was only ever going to be a 7 out of 10? Darren responded by sending me regular text messages throughout the next day: 'I love you when you're shrill.'

I couldn't put it off any longer. We had a deadline, and once all the characters had been recorded Bruce still needed to mix the master copy and create a soundtrack of background noise and scene creation. That would take at least a week and time was running out, so I needed to stop avoiding it and just record. In some ways, Joanna was the most important character – she was the narrator. I wrote the manuscript using her voice as the question in the beginning and the answer in the end. She began the story on Easter Saturday (in a grieving, disbelieving sort of way) and then she sat and listened to each of the other characters tell their version of the promise (and the faithfulness of God), until time passed and she finished her story after an impossible Easter Sunday, and a life-changing Pentecost.

So if Joanna didn't set the scene and the pace and the story, we couldn't do it. It wouldn't work without her, and I had to be her. The publisher had requested that I be her because they thought my voice would set up the connection with the listeners. So on 6 August, I went to the studio. Mel came too, for moral support. I had a glass of water and I went into the linen cupboard. I tried to slow down and pause and imagine that I was talking to someone, that I wasn't in a linen cupboard and I wasn't hopeless. But it didn't work. It was pretty dreadful. I didn't even need to look at Bruce to know that he thought I was still a 7 out of 10. I wasn't good enough and I never would be. I came back out and we all sighed. We had more cups of tea and we prayed.

Then I got up and went back in again. 'Try to project your voice a bit more deliberately,' said Bruce through the head-phones. Then he paused for a while. 'Actually, do you know anyone who's a bit deaf?' he asked. 'Or someone who can't hear you very well; someone to whom you speak very clearly and deliberately?'

'Yes,' I said through the sound system, 'my grandma. She's 99 and she uses a hearing loop. She studies English literature at university and she reads thirty books a year.'

'Good,' said Bruce. 'Read it for Grandma.'

I did. I stood in the linen cupboard and I pictured Grandma. I could see her at the dining table with the grapes, the choco-late biscuits and the lemon biscuits. I could hear the noise of the china cups as she poured the tea. I could hear her voice and see her curly white hair and the way she frowned when she couldn't hear what I was saying. So I calmed down and spoke very clearly and deliberately and lovingly to Grandma. My legs shook and I lost track of time, but I desperately wan-ted her to hear the story and the message, because it was com-pelling, important and life-changing.

'That was much better,' said Bruce after the second chapter. 'It was even good.'

I almost collapsed.

The next week we submitted the master copy of the audio to the publisher and we started preparing for the book launch. That was exciting! I hand delivered invitations to all the local churches and we formed a catering team. We met on our back deck and talked about lamb kofta balls and semolina syrup cake. But even more exciting than the food was the perform-ance itself. We planned to showcase the audio version, with four of the readers dressing up in costume and performing snippets of the work on stage while the audio played. In between the snippets I would be the narrator of the show and bring the message to life through the centuries and the characters. We spent hours practising the script and planning special lighting, props, sound effects and costumes. The anticipation was intense. The boys all listened patiently to the script on our CD player (over and over again) and they offered occasional suggestions and feedback.

'Why does the Singer sound like she's in a temple?' asked Chris.

'And how old was Noah's wife really?' asked Stephen.

'And when are we going on holiday?' asked Jeremy.

I smiled. 'After the launch,' I said, finding it difficult to believe that there was going to be a time when the launch would be over.

In the week running up to the launch the anticipation increased and various family members arrived, all bringing their own expectations.

The evening itself didn't begin very well. The auditorium was nice and clean but something went wrong with the door of the ladies' toilet. It mysteriously became locked and no one was able to get in. Nat ran off looking for the cleaner, in the middle of trying to become Mary Magdalene. Then our friends from church started setting up chairs for 300 people. I kept looking at them and feeling horribly nervous. What if only thirty people came? I might never recover from the humiliation.

'Do you think we could hide some of the chairs and then sneak them out if we don't need them – when no one's looking?' I asked. They ignored me.

Just after that, the entire sound and lighting system went down, quite spectacularly, with a loud noise from somewhere near the ceiling. We all looked up at the place where sound and lighting usually comes from.

'Oh dear!' Nat groaned. It was moments before we were due to have our final quick rehearsal on stage.

'Right,' I suggested, 'shall we just pretend?'

Instead of pretending, we prayed. And slowly, the people started arriving – exactly 300 of them. Then the sound came back on and the lights worked and the toilet door opened. I was invited on to the stage by our pastor, who welcomed the crowd and began the initial interview. He started by asking me about the process of writing the book and what I had enjoyed the most. I began to tell them how I loved the tangible nature of the writing and the sense of walking through the places where the women walked. As I was speaking, I noticed that the receiver part of my radio mic was disappearing down the back of my trousers. When I'd put it on I'd found that the clip was missing, so I had tucked it into the waist of my trousers, which was fine while I was walking around the hall, but not fine now that I was sitting on the stage in front of 300 people. I kept answering his questions and smiling, while imagining what would happen when I eventually stood up. What if the whole thing disappeared down my trouser leg and then the weight of it caused the mic to fly off into space?

'And what did you find most helpful personally as you were writing *The Promise*?' the pastor asked.

'Well,' I answered, still imagining the flight of my mic, 'the one thing that really stood out to me was the promise of God to his people, over and over again, "I will be with you." It's incredible that he said it to Abraham and then Isaac, Jacob, Moses, Joshua, Gideon, David, Solomon, Jeremiah and the exiles, and all the way through the Old Testament until, amazingly, in Zechariah 2:10 he says, "Shout and be glad, O Daughter of Zion. For I am coming, and I will live among you." And he came! God sent his own son, Jesus, to live amongst us, and even more amazingly, he sent his Spirit to live *within* us, to change us and to mould us and to get us ready for that place where he'll always be with us.'

My mic was still in situ and the audience were still listening, so I kept speaking.

'For me, the message has been striking. In the beginning, I kept wondering why the Israelites needed to hear it so often. Didn't they already know he was with them? Wasn't it already obvious from the pillar of smoke, the tabernacle, the burning bush, the manna, the prophets and the cloud arriving in the temple? Why did they need to keep hearing the same promise over and over again?

'But then I thought about myself. Why do I need to keep hearing it? Isn't it obvious to me? I have the Scriptures and the truth of the resurrection and the certainty of the Holy Spirit and a life of moments where God has been revealing himself to me. So why do I need to keep hearing it? Because I do, daily.

'You see, we arrived back from Nepal three years ago and ever since then I've been struggling with a sense of home. I've been feeling as if I'm in between worlds or that I'm lost between the two of them. I've been asking all sorts of questions about purpose and meaning and identity. Even when things have been clear and wonderful, even when the publisher has been communicating, and even when my family and the back deck and the *dal bhat* have all been delightful, I've still had all these questions, an inner longing for home or a greater sense of belonging. But he keeps bringing me back to his promise, "I will be with you." He will be with me in Iraq and the Blue Mountains and Dhulikhel, and on the aeroplane and at the hospital and in the prison in Fiji. He will be with me in the earthquake and the break-in, at the funeral and the launch, at the radio interview, and all the days in between when I'm boring, repetitive, insecure, tired and miserable. He will be with me. That's the promise, the only promise.

'And the promise makes all the difference. Maybe the reason we need to keep hearing it is because the temptation to think that we've been abandoned is so very strong, for all of us. When the seasons are hard, when nothing works as it should, when illness comes and stays, when relationships are difficult or when our loved ones are a long way away and we fall between worlds, it's really hard. We struggle. But God is still with us. He'll never leave us. And because he's with us, he makes us at home, wherever we are – because *he* is home. We're at home in him and he makes everywhere home. *The Message* even translates John 15 in exactly those words. Jesus said to his disciples, "Make your home in me just as I do in you." (John 15:4). It's a command! It's one of the last things Jesus said to his disciples before his arrest. So we need to keep asking ourselves what it means for us to make our home in him? And we all put so much energy into creating nice, comfortable homes for ourselves here but what does it mean to make our home in him? What would it be like to put all of that same energy into making our home in him? What if we were to find all our identity and familiarity and acceptance and purpose in him, regardless of our surroundings? And what if we actually realised, moment by moment, that this home here is only temporary, that it's not going to last, that it's going to fade away . . . and there's a true home coming – that place with him where we'll never feel like the outsider ever again, and we'll never fall between worlds and we'll never feel weak or hopeless ever again. He's with us. That's it. That's what I've learnt.'

Graham smiled and spoke again. He asked me about the audio version of the book, so I introduced it and then I stood up to introduce the characters and their stories. My mic stayed in place. My voice stayed controlled – well, it wasn't smooth but it wasn't shrill. And the characters spoke and we moved in time from Noah's wife in the flood, to Rahab in the city of Jericho, to Abigail in the palace, and to Mary Magdalene at the tomb.

'Imagine this,' Mary Magdalene said. 'What if something happened on that cross yesterday which meant that our sins have been dealt with for all time? What if we never have to offer a goat again? What if we're really forgiven? Imagine . . .'

I walked past Mary Magdalene and to the front of the stage as the lights went down and I *imagined* it.

It was a perfect evening. If I was in Nepal I would have called it *ramailo*. And then I'd explain to you that *ramailo* means something has been very good – in every sense of the word. It's the word you use when absolutely everything is good – the food, the company, the friends, the conversation, the sense of belonging, the connection, the message and the hope for the future.

Lord, we thank you that you're with us. We thank you that you tell us to make our home in you and that changes everything. And even as we speak of home, we start to imagine pot plants and colours and curtains and kitchens . . . but it's something bigger than that as well. As soon as we say the word home, it's like we breathe out and feel our shoulders relax. We take off our shoes and put the kettle on and feel the comfort of the known and the familiar. We feel the sense of security and peace and purpose, and we know we can only find it in you . . . and that once we've found it in you, we'll know home everywhere – even on the aeroplane and in the earthquake and beside the hospital bed and on the telephone – because you're with us everywhere.

But we especially pray today that in our homes right now, you would keep teaching us. Keep showing us that you'll use our weaknesses and our frailties. We don't have to be perfect or a 10 out of 10 every time, we just have to get up and keep walking and keep loving you. Remind us what it means to give 100 per cent of what you've given us to give rather than needing to be 100 per cent every time. And Lord, when we start to lose perspective, when we start to cling on too tightly to perfection or the physical things around us, show us again, deeply and gently, that they're temporary, that they won't last forever. That they're merely the beginning of the forever story, where we'll see you and know you face to face. Thank you.

Amen

24

HE WHO IS COMING

The next week, we went on holiday. Jeremy couldn't quite believe it. We packed the bags, the dog and the fishing tackle, and we drove three hours south to our favourite spot at Jervis Bay. The breeze was gentle on the water. The seagulls perched on the jetty, their bodies preparing for flight. We unpacked the car and I eased myself into a comfy chair by the biggest window in the house, where I could watch the waves move from the left-hand side of the channel to the right. I felt the sun warm on my back. Darren turned on some music and rummaged around in his bag for his Nepali language book. It's always a good time to learn some more Nepali language, he said. I listened to the boys as they collected their balls and their bikes from the car. I relaxed my shoulders and thought that I might never move again.

Somebody told me once that performing for a crowd was a bit like jumping out of an aeroplane. You become the fullest blown-up version of yourself. You fill your parachute with air until it's the biggest and brightest and most glorious version of you. Then, after an incredible and life-changing flight, you have to land back on the hard ground and pack your parachute away into a very small backpack. You can't walk around in your normal life with your parachute fully open (because it would drive you and your family crazy), so you pack it away carefully and firmly. And sometimes the packing away can feel a bit tiresome and as if you're running out of air. During the next three days I felt the adrenaline slowly seep out of me and into the grains of sand on the beach and the dishwashing suds in the sink and the books that we read together. I dealt the cards for the boys, stared at the numbers, helped with the puzzle, and held on to Millie while they chased crabs along the beach. For part of the time I was tempted to wonder what I should do next, or write next, or perform next, or become next . . . but I resisted it. Just sit where you are, I told myself. Feel the grass, watch the pelicans, listen to the wind in the trees and taste that early morning cup of tea.

We did that for four days. Then on Wednesday morning the phone rang. It was my brother ringing from Sydney. He said that Grandma had died in the night, aged 99½. They had found her that morning in her reading chair in the retirement village in Canberra, with her last book by her side, *The Promise*. She'd gone home.

I put the phone down and shared the news with Darren and the boys. Then I went and sat on the jetty and pulled out my Bible. I turned to Hebrews and read the same passage that I had read in Pokhara 16 years earlier:

> All these people were still living by faith when they died. They did not receive the things promised; they only saw them and welcomed them from a distance. And they admitted that they were aliens and strangers on earth. People who say such things show that they are looking for a country of their own. If they had been thinking of the country they had left, they would have had opportunity to return. Instead, they were longing for a better country – a heavenly one. Therefore God is not ashamed to be called their God, for he has prepared a city for them. (Heb. 11:13–16)

Steve had said that wherever we are – in England, Australia, Germany or Hong Kong – we're aliens and strangers. We're not at home because 'home' is something different altogether. It's the thing we long for. Home is being with God, and in God, and longing to be with him forever. And maybe if we really understood that, it would change the way we lived forever.

I looked back at the water and thought again about Grandma, glancing back at Hebrews chapter 10. We've *been made holy* through the sacrifice of Jesus – once and for all. We've been made 10s. We don't need any more burnt offerings or sin offerings or priests performing religious duties at the temple. We don't need any more righteous acts. All our sins and lawless acts have been dealt with at the cross and are remembered no more. Therefore, we can draw near to God, in full assurance of faith, spur each other on, remember the earlier days, live by faith, persevere . . . because 'he who is coming will come and will not delay' (Heb. 10:37).

That's why. That's the reason. 'He who is coming will come and will not delay.' That's why we get out of bed and eat breakfast and walk to the shops and the school and the train station and the hospital. Because he who is coming will come and not delay. He's coming back and we are waiting for his return – more than we're waiting for the baby or the degree or the wedding or the grandchild or the job or the renovated house that will finally make us feel like we're at home. He's coming back and we're waiting for his return.

I looked around me at the water and the jetty and the boys on their bikes. Then I remembered the email from my friend. Maybe the gift of being between homes is such that it causes us to face our homelessness. We're not at home yet because we're on the way. We *want* to be at home but we're not there yet (none of us), and sometimes the questions we have during the in between force us to consider what home really is. We're not there yet but we're heading home. And within all of that longing and questioning we sit down and say thank you for the cost he bore to make us his and to prepare a place and a home for us. A place where we'll finally be at home, and where the sound of weeping and crying and sibling squabbles and raised voices will be no more, where the wolf and lamb will feed together, where all mankind will come and bow down before the Lord.

So Naomi, in the meantime live like it matters, live like you're longing for it, live like you're preparing for it, live like there's a day marked in red after which there won't be any more chances and there won't be any more longing. Live like you're heading home, because *'he who is coming, will come and will not delay.'*

At that moment Jeremy came rushing back down from the house towards me with his hands cupped together.

'Look Mum!' he said, arriving at the jetty out of breath and talking too quickly. Then he slowly opened his hands towards me. A perfect yellow butterfly lay on the palm of his right hand. Its wings were golden and smooth. There were tiny black dots near the centre. We were both quiet as we stared at it. Then the butterfly gently lifted its wings and flew away. First of all, it flew to the edge of the jetty and it landed there for a while. It shone in the sunlight. Then it flew off to another place behind the gum trees. We watched it go.

Sometimes, for some seasons we're like the butterfly. We alight in beautiful places and we make them home for a while. The places and the people and the roles are a gift. We grow to love them and understand them. The associations are kind and they're to be treasured, so we hold out our hands and say thank you, because in those homes and places there are things to do and truths to learn and people to love dearly. And we know that in all of those places we are home because of who we are in Christ. But during the whole time, wherever we are (and no matter how well we know it), there's a small part of us that is still the alien and the stranger, that is still longing for something more deeply satisfying. It's as if the longing creeps up from deep inside us, and it sees and welcomes things from a distance. The deepest part of us, the quietest part of us lives by faith. And that's how it should be, because at the right time, in the right season and in the right chapter, we'll make the journey home, to the place so lovingly prepared for us.

Oh Lord, today we remember again. We remember who you are and what you've done for us and what you're preparing for us – a home forever. And we thank you. We're looking forward to it. We can't wait.

Even now, we sit here and try to imagine that place without anger or fear or tears, a place where we'll never feel nervous or worried or insecure again, a place where we'll be with you, where the borders that separate us as societies will have gone and your people will be together giving you honour forever – singing a new song. Thank you. Help us to long for it.

But in the meantime, help us to also respond in praise, in thanks, in obedience and in perseverance and love in the place you have put us for now. Help us to say, 'Lord, here I am, use me today in this place, for the sake of your name, until you come again.'

And we pray all of this in the name of Jesus, but we don't speak his name lightly, or as if it's a name we always say. We speak it with awe and wonder and tears.

Amen

Trust me. There is plenty of room for you in my Father's home. If that weren't so, would I have told you that I'm on my way to get a room ready for you? And if I'm on my way to get your room ready, I'll come back and get you so you can live where I live. And you already know the road I'm taking.
(John 14:1–4, *The Message*)

GLOSSARY

Achar – pickle
Bideshi – foreigner
Chappals – sandals
Chiya – a sweet milky tea drink
Dahi – yoghurt
Dal bhat – rice and lentils forming the traditional Nepali meal
Doko – a cane basket carried on the back
Jili kurdi – traditional Kurdish women's clothing
Kurta surwal – knee length dress worn by Nepali women with
    trousers underneath
Mo-mo – spicy meat wrapped in a dumpling pastry
Namlo – a flat piece of woven rope worn round the forehead
    that the people of Nepal use to carry loads
Pandhra rupiya – fifteen rupees
Ramailo – very good
Tikcha – OK
Tuk-tuk – a small three-wheeled vehicle

BOOK CLUB QUESTIONS

1. In what ways do you identify with Naomi's journey?
2. If possible, describe a time in your life when you have felt a sense of being in between homes or roles.
3. Naomi's friend emailed her and suggested that being in between homes and roles and ministries is a gift. Do you agree? How have you found this to be so?
4. During your in between times, were there truths and Bible passages that particularly helped you?
5. If your current stage of life feels more settled or connected, how does the phrase 'aliens and strangers' continue to challenge you?
6. At the beginning of chapter 5, Naomi described a more appropriate answer to the question 'What will you do in Australia?' as 'I'll be the clay . . . and I'll remember who the Potter is.' How does remembering who 'the Potter' is impact the decisions you are making today?
7. Do you ever think back wistfully to previous seasons (or communities) and wish you were back there? How can you grow in appreciating the place (and the people) amongst whom God has you right now?
8. How does the assurance that 'He who is coming will come and will not delay' (Heb 10:37) specifically impact the way you live today?

For more information regarding Naomi's writing and speaking ministry, please visit her website www.NaomiReed.Info and join 'My Seventh Monsoon' on Facebook.

Naomi supports the work of the International Nepal Fellowship, a Christian mission serving Nepali people through health and development work. For more information go to www.inf.org

INTERNATIONAL NEPAL FELLOWSHIP

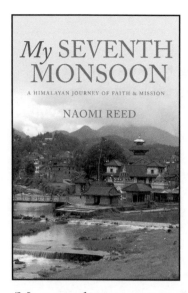

My Seventh Monsoon

A Himalayan Journey of Faith & Mission

Naomi Reed

'My seventh monsoon was the hardest of them all. I sat on the back porch of our Himalayan home and stared as the rain streamed down all around me. I had never felt so hemmed in – by the constant rain, by the effects of the civil war and by the demands of home-school. As I sat there and listened to the pounding on our tin roof, I wondered whether I would make it through. I wondered whether I could cope with another 120 days of rain. And in doing so, I began to long for another season . . .'

From the view point of her seventh monsoon, Naomi Reed takes time to look back on the seasons of her life. As she does so, she shares with us her journey of faith and mission and reveals poignant truths about God and the way he works his purposes in our lives through seasons.

978-1-86024-828-3

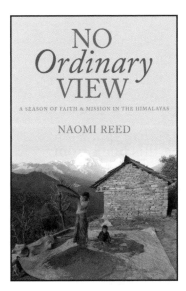

No Ordinary View

A Season of Faith & Mission in the Himalayas

Naomi Reed

'The Himalayan view from our back porch was normally breath-taking, but that day I sat there and wondered. Ten years of civil war, a deteriorating health system, an economic crisis and a political stalemate. It was a background of hopelessness for the lives of our Nepali friends and the community that we lived in. In such a setting of pain and darkness, how could God reveal his nature? And how could he call me by name? I wasn't sure. I didn't think it was possible.'

From within the uncertainty of Nepal's civil war, Naomi continues the story of her family's desire to train Nepali physiotherapists and share God's love in word and action. Her honesty and genuine longing to see God's purposes and sovereignty make this unforgettable reading.

978-1-86024-843-6

Authentic

We trust you enjoyed reading this book from
Authentic Media.
If you want to be informed of
any new titles from this author and other exciting
releases you can sign up to the Authentic
newsletter online:

www.authenticmedia.co.uk

Contact us

By Post: Authentic Media
52 Presley Way
Crownhill
Milton Keynes
MK8 0ES

E-mail: info@authenticmedia.co.uk

Follow us: